DISCARD

SILENCING THE DEMON'S ADVOCATE

SILENCING THE DEMON'S ADVOCATE

The Strategy of Descartes' Meditations

Ronald Rubin

STANFORD UNIVERSITY PRESS

STANFORD, CALIFORNIA

2008

Stanford University Press
Stanford, California

Printed in the United States of America
on acid-free, archival-quality paper

Library of Congress Cataloging-in-Publication Data

Rubin, Ronald.
    Silencing the demon's advocate : the strategy of Descartes' Meditations /
Ronald Rubin.
        p.   cm.
    Includes bibliographical references and index.
    ISBN 978-0-8047-5816-1 (cloth : alk. paper)
    1. Descartes, René, 1596–1650. Meditationes de prima philosophia.   I. Title.
B1854.R83 2008
194—dc22

                                                        2007038389

Contents

For Susan

Acknowledgments

So many people contributed to this book that I won't try to thank them individually. I will, however, mention two to whom I am especially indebted for their thoughtful reviews: Lawrence Nolan and Allen Wood. Although their comments have caused many changes, I'm sure that much remains with which they disagree, and I of course accept full responsibility for the errors that remain.

I am also grateful to John Perry for his advice and encouragement.

My thanks to Pitzer College, whose policies on released time and computer support have cleared my way.

And, finally, thanks to my wife, Susan Perry, without whose support this project would never have been completed—or, indeed, started.

Preface

The main line of reasoning in Descartes' *Meditations*[1] seems to fit a pattern familiar from Euclidean geometry: Descartes seems to begin from simple, self-evident propositions and to deduce the conclusions of the *Meditations* from those propositions in the way that Euclid deduces theorems from axioms and postulates. Descartes himself seems to suggest this "geometric" interpretation of his reasoning when, at the end of *Replies II,* he lays out the arguments of the *Meditations* "in the manner of a geometry" [*more geometrico*] (AT 7:160–70).[2]

Yet those who view Descartes as trying to move from self-evident axioms to certain conclusions through straightforward deductive reasoning face at least six problems:

First, there is the riddle of the Cogito. When Descartes tries to establish the certainty of "I am" in *Meditation II,* is he presenting that proposition as an axiom or as a theorem? If as an axiom, why does he frequently describe the movement from "I think" to "I am" as an inference? On the other hand, if he presents "I am" as a theorem, what exactly are the axioms from which he deduces it, why does he deem those axioms more certain than the propositions that he explicitly called into doubt in *Meditation I,* and how can it be that he takes the theorem "I am"—rather than the axioms from which he deduced that theorem—as the single "immovable point" on which he builds his system?

Second, there is Descartes' explicit avowal that his method is not the same as that used in geometry. Near the end of *Replies II* (AT 7:155–59), after carefully distinguishing "analytic method" from "synthetic method" and noting that traditional geometry follows the synthetic method, he states that, in the *Meditations,* his method was analytic. (While he does go on to present some of the central arguments of the *Meditations* in "geometrical fashion" [AT 7:160–70], he does so reluctantly, cautioning that his synthetic presentation is not an adequate substitute for what happens in the *Meditations* themselves [AT 7:159].)

Third, there is the problem of explaining Descartes' insistence that he makes use of doubt to establish his conclusions. (See, for example, *The Search for Truth* [AT 2:522].) Although geometric proofs might go some way toward settling doubts, it's difficult, if not impossible, to see how doubt might contribute to those proofs.

Fourth, there is the problem of explaining why Descartes believed himself to be justified in taking such propositions as "There is at least as much reality in a cause as in its effect" as axioms when attempting to prove that God exists. Such premises don't seem any more obviously true than propositions like "$2 + 3 = 5$," but, in *Meditation I,* he insists that these simple propositions are subject to doubt and hence that he ought to treat them as if he knew them to be false. (If he takes himself to apprehend these premises clearly and distinctly, he might be able to justify his accepting them by appeal to the principle, established in *Meditation IV,* that whatever he clearly and distinctly apprehends is true. But, because he derived this principle directly from the claim that God exists, such a justification would apparently be unacceptably circular.)

Fifth, there is a problem of circularity concerning the reasoning in *Meditation V.* Apparently, having established "God exists" as a theorem in *Meditation III,* and having deduced the proposition "Whatever we clearly and distinctly apprehend is true" as a corollary of that theorem, Descartes uses that corollary in *Meditation V* as a premise of an argument to the conclusion that God exists. If the reasoning of the *Meditations* does fit the pattern of a formal geometry, it seems undeniable that he has committed the blunder of having deduced a theorem directly from itself.

Sixth, there is an overarching problem concerning Descartes' views on the certainty of mathematics and geometry. While he does say in *Meditation I* that the propositions of arithmetic and geometry are more certain than other propositions that he believes, he does not there say, or even suggest, that he is perfectly certain of their truth. On the contrary, in *Meditation I,* he explicitly demonstrates that he has grounds for doubts concerning even these propositions, concluding that "*nothing that* [he] used to believe is beyond legitimate doubt" (AT 7:20). In *Meditation III*, he seems to use "2 + 3 = 5" as an example of a proposition of whose truth he is uncertain (AT 7:36), and in *Meditation V*, he says that, under certain circumstances, he can have doubts about the Euclidean theorem "The internal angles of a triangle equal two right angles" (AT 7:69). But, if Descartes views mathematics and geometry as themselves uncertain, why would he think that, by proceeding in a straightforwardly geometric manner, he could establish propositions of "first philosophy" with perfect certainty?

All six of these problems have the same origin: the assumption that Descartes attempts to become perfectly certain of propositions, such as "God exists," by garnering new and better support for those propositions. I will challenge that assumption. Descartes calls his beliefs into doubt in *Meditation I* by producing grounds for doubt concerning those beliefs. Regardless of the quantity or strength of the support that he can produce in favor of those beliefs, he cannot become perfectly certain of their truth until he somehow nullifies those grounds. Accordingly, his strategy in *Meditations I* through *IV* is not to *add* support for his beliefs such as "God exists," but to *subtract* grounds for doubt.

But is the thought that Descartes' method is subtractive incompatible with the view that his reasoning fits the geometric model? His grounds for doubt concerning the beliefs with which he begins the *Meditations* are provided by hypotheses that he considers in *Meditation I*—and apparently his method for refuting these hypotheses is to begin from self-evident axioms, deduce that a veracious God exists, and infer as a corollary that the doubt-producing hypotheses of *Meditation I* are false. Then can't we say both that Descartes proceeds in a geometric manner and that he becomes certain by subtracting grounds for doubt?

I think not. As I will argue, Descartes does not neutralize the doubt-producing hypotheses of *Meditation I* by showing them to be false. Rather, by constructing various arguments in *Meditations II* through *VI*, he tries to work himself into a position from which these hypotheses no longer make sense to him. The strategy seems counterintuitive because we generally expect continued study to expand the range of our understanding rather than to narrow it—but the strategy is, I will suggest, acceptable. A hypothesis can serve as grounds for doubt only if it seems coherent, and clarification of concepts can sometimes reveal to us that hypotheses that once seemed plausible are in fact nonsense.

That Descartes adopted this strategy is revealed, I will argue, by what he writes in the *Meditations*. In part, however, my case for the subtractive interpretation will be philosophical rather then textual. If we accept the usual interpretation of *Meditations,* we must view the problems that I have sketched as unsolvable—and we must therefore view Descartes' strategy as fundamentally flawed. On the other hand, as I will show, if we take the reasoning of the *Meditations* to be aimed at revealing the incoherence (rather than the falsity) of various doubt-producing hypotheses, the strategic knots that I have outlined—including the problems of circularity—loosen.

To lay the foundation for the explication of Descartes' strategy, I will offer analyses of two notions of doubt and outline Descartes' reasons for saying that he has grounds for doubt concerning each of his beliefs (Chapter 1). Next I will examine the aim that Descartes sets for himself in the *Meditations*: perfect certainty (Chapter 2). Descartes insists that, to attain this end, he must isolate himself from the influence of his previous beliefs, and he therefore begins writing in a fictitious voice—the voice of someone who has the same experiences as he does and regards the same reasoning as valid, but who believes that he is dreaming and that his mind is the product of an evil demon. For convenience, I will view this voice as belonging to someone distinct from Descartes, whom I will call the Demon's Advocate (Chapter 3). Descartes' primary rule of method early in the *Meditations* is, I will argue, to accept a proposition into his system of belief if and only if he can convince the Advocate of its truth.

For purposes of convincing the Demon's Advocate, straightforward argument would be useless. If Descartes were to construct a compelling argument to the conclusion that 2 + 3 = 5, for example, the Advocate would have an easy reply. "In view of your argument," he might say to Descartes, "it seems undeniably true to me that 2 + 3 = 5. But my mind is so poorly designed that what seems most obviously true to me is in fact false. So the proposition '2 + 3 = 5' must be false." Understandably, faced with the possibility of such a reply, Descartes wonders whether he will be able to convince the Demon's Advocate of anything. But, early in

Meditation II, he does find a way to convince the Advocate of the truth of the proposition "I am" (Chapter 4). As I will show, although this way does involve Descartes' inferring "I am" from the doubt-producing hypotheses of *Meditation I*, he performs this inference to reveal a relation of entailment between propositions, not to prove that "I am" is true in the usual sense of *prove*.

Just as Descartes does not offer the argument of *Meditation II* to provide confirmation for the proposition "I am," he does not construct the theological arguments of *Meditation III* to demonstrate the truth of the proposition "God exists." On the interpretation of these arguments that I will offer (Chapters 5 and 6), their function is to compel our Wills to affirm the proposition "God exists," thereby leaving us unable to entertain various doubt-producing hypotheses. (At the end of Chapter 6, I will reply to the objection that, if I were right about this, the program of the *Meditations* would amount to nothing more than psychological trickery.)

Armed with the reasoning of *Meditation III*, Descartes thinks that he can deprive the Demon's Advocate of one of his foundational beliefs—namely, the belief that his mind is the product of an evil demon. For this reason, after *Meditation IV*, the primary rule of Descartes' method changes from "Accept a proposition into your system of belief if and only if you can convince the Demon's Advocate of its truth" to "Accept a proposition into your system of belief if and only if you clearly and distinctly apprehend it" (Chapter 7). Descartes' first application of this rule, which occurs in *Meditation V*, has to do with the proposition "God exists" (Chapter 8). As I will argue, although Descartes establishes this rule because he believes that God exists, his application of the rule to the proposition "God exists" does not involve him in circular reasoning.

Finally, I will look at the central arguments of *Meditation VI*. An investigation of Descartes' argument for mind-body dualism (Chapter 9) will show that the device of the Demon's Advocate is at work even at this late stage of the project, and an examination of his "proof" of the existence of physical objects (Chapter 10) will reveal how he tries, without entirely abandoning his initial aims, to set the method of the *Meditations* aside and return to commonplace standards of evidence.

SILENCING THE DEMON'S ADVOCATE

CHAPTER I

Doubt

With the title of *Meditation I,* Descartes poses a question: What can I call into doubt? By the end of *Meditation I,* he has arrived at a definite answer: "I'm forced to admit," he announces, "that nothing I used to believe is beyond legitimate doubt" (AT 7:21).

The announcement is paradoxical. Descartes himself says—both in the *Meditations* (for instance, at AT 7:36) and in the *Objections and Replies* (for instance, at AT 7:145)—that we see the truth of some propositions so clearly that we can't prevent ourselves from affirming them. Then how can he deny that, when he begins the *Meditations,* he is certain of their truth? And, if he is certain of their truth, how can he claim to have called them in doubt?

As I will argue, the paradox rests, at least in part, on confusion concerning Descartes' use of the phrase "call into doubt." After examining this use, I will argue that Descartes has plausible reasons for thinking that the reasoning of *Meditation I* calls both his empirical beliefs and his nonempirical beliefs into doubt. While I don't deny that this reasoning has its problems, my discussion will reveal that Descartes' position is more credible than it might initially seem.

Reversing what might seem a more natural order, I will postpone until the next chapter the question of why Descartes regards his ability to call his beliefs into doubt important or interesting. Here my aims are simply to clarify what he means when he concludes that he can call all of his beliefs into doubt and to trace the path that leads him to that conclusion.

"Doubting-That" and "Having-Doubts-About"

Stepping back for a moment from the text of the *Meditations,* I will devote this section to the examination of two importantly different forms of doubting. Although the analyses of these forms will be indefinite (at points that I will note), they will provide a basis for the explication of Descartes' strategy to follow.

Consider (English) expressions in which *doubt* is used as a verb—expressions of the form "*A* doubts that *p*," where "*A*" holds the place of a personal name and "*p*" that of a clause. In particular, consider "John doubts that it is raining." On a given occasion of its use, this sentence is true only if the person denoted (on that occasion) by the name *John* has thought about whether it is raining; we don't doubt what we have never considered.[1] Also, the sentence is true only if John neither believes that it is raining nor believes that it is not raining; we would contradict ourselves by saying either "John doubts that it's raining but he believes that it's raining" or "John doubts that it's raining but he believes that it's not raining."

Generalizing from this example, we can identify an activity that I will call *doubting-that:*

1.1. To say that *A* doubts that *p* is just to say that, while *A* has thought about whether it's the case that *p, A* neither believes that *p* nor believes that not-*p*.

Etymology concurs: the term *doubt* derives from the Latin verb *dubare,* meaning "to vacillate," and doubting-that involves wavering between affirmation and denial. (When one of the characters in Berkeley's dialogues asks whether doubting "consists in embracing the affirmative or the negative side of a question," another plausibly replies, "In neither; for whoever understands English cannot but know that doubting signifies a suspense between both.")[2]

Of course, if an athlete says, "I'll run a mile in three minutes," a coach might reply, "I doubt it!" even though the coach firmly believes that the athlete will not be able to do what he or she has claimed. But is this a bone fide case of doubt? Or is the verb *to doubt* used here out of politeness, merely to cushion the blow of direct denial? I would say that, despite the idiomatic correctness of what the coach says, he or she is not truly in doubt at all. Indeed, the coach is certain that the athlete will not be able to what he or she has predicted, and (in a way to be detailed in the next chapter) certainty is the opposite of doubt.

Still, aren't there cases in which people doubt what they believe? Suppose, for instance, that, when Susan asks a friend where Cleveland is, the friend replies by saying that it's on Lake Erie. Suppose that Susan comes to believe, solely on the basis of the friend's testimony, that Cleveland is on Lake Erie. Finally, suppose that Susan hears a rumor that her friend is a habitual liar—a rumor that she does not believe but that she is unwilling completely to rule out. If her suspicions are not sufficiently strong to induce her to abandon her belief about Cleveland's location, she might say, "I believe that Cleveland is on Lake Erie, but I have some doubts about it." With the first clause of this sentence, she announces that she holds a certain belief, and, with the second, that she holds the belief in a certain way—namely, tentatively and with reservations.

While this story does illustrate the general truth that doubt is somehow compatible with belief, it does not provide any reason for saying that a sentence of the form "*A* believes that *p*" is consistent with the corresponding sentence of the form "*A* doubts that *p*." As long as Susan believes that Cleveland is on Lake Erie, she does not doubt that it is there, even if her belief is tentative. What the story does show is that a sentence of the form "*A* believes that *p*" is consistent with the corresponding sentence of the form "*A* has doubts about its being the case that *p*." We might subsume both doubting-that and having-doubts-about under the general rubric of doubting, but the two forms differ from one another, notably in how they relate to believing: that *A* doubts that *p* entails that *A* does not believe that *p*, but *A* may have doubts about its being the case that *p* even if *A* does believe that *p*.

For reasons that will emerge, the concept of having-doubts-about is somewhat unclear. We might, however, capture the central idea like this:

1.2. To say that a person *A* has doubts about its being the case that *p* is to say that *A* has in mind a hypothesis "*h*" such that (i) *A* has some suspicion that *h* and (ii) *A* sees that "*h*" somehow challenges his or her belief that *p*.[3]

In the story about Susan, the belief that *p* is of course the belief that Cleveland is on Lake Erie, and the hypothesis is that her friend is a habitual liar. It seems obvious that, in the relevant sense of *challenge*, this hypothesis does challenge her belief. But what in general does it mean to say that a hypothesis challenges a belief?

There are, I suggest, at least two ways in which the consideration of a hypothesis might challenge a person's belief:

First, a hypothesis might directly challenge *A*'s belief that *p*—that is, perhaps in conjunction with some of *A*'s beliefs, the hypothesis might imply that it's not the case that *p*. Imagine, for example that, although a juror in a trial believes a defendant to be guilty, the defense attorney has presented a rival theory of the crime that the juror cannot completely rule out. Here, a certain hypothesis (namely, that the crime happened in the way the defense attorney claims) directly challenges the belief that the defendant is guilty: the defense's theory of the crime—together, perhaps, with other propositions that the juror believes, such as the belief that only one person committed the crime in question—entails that the defendant is not guilty.[4]

Second, a hypothesis "*h*" might indirectly challenge *A*'s belief that *p*—that is, although "*h*" is itself compatible with "*p*," the acceptance of "*h*" might leave *A* without any reason for believing that *p*. This is, I suggest, what happens in the example about Cleveland. Accepting the hypothesis that what her friend says is unreliable would not force Susan to believe that Cleveland is not on Lake Erie, since even the worst liars sometimes tell the truth. Yet there is a fairly clear point to saying that the hypothesis somehow challenges her belief: since her only reason for believing that Cleveland is on Lake Erie is that her friend has told her so, she will no longer have a good reason for believing that Cleveland is on Lake Erie if she accepts the hypothesis as true (provided, of course, that she has no special reason for believing that her friend told the truth on this occasion).

Sometimes hypotheses that challenge beliefs indirectly are about instruments whose use led to the belief's acquisition. Think, for example, about the machine that bank clerks use to test bills for genuineness. When a clerk places a bill into the machine (let's suppose), the machine responds sometimes with a green light to indicate that the bill is genuine and sometimes with a red light to indicate that the bill is counterfeit. Imagine that, at first, a certain clerk uses the machine unreflectively, simply accepting that when the red light goes on the bill in the machine is counterfeit. One day the clerk might notice that he cannot fully justify his confidence. "I believe that the machine is properly designed," he says to himself, "but—not having any definite idea about how it works or who designed it—I have some slight suspicion that it may not be accurate." If we assume that the machine provides the clerk with his only evidence that a given bill is counterfeit, a hypothesis about an instrument (namely, the hypothesis that the machine is poorly designed) indirectly challenges a belief (namely, the belief that the bill is counterfeit) that was acquired through the use of that instrument.

Even if the clerk suspects that the hypothesis may be true and sees that it (indirectly) challenges his belief that *p*, he might reasonably believe both that the machine is properly designed and that the bill is in fact counterfeit. Thus, having doubts about its being the case that *p* does not require either subscribing to a hypothesis that challenges the belief that *p* or abandoning the belief that *p*. All that is required for having doubts about its being the case that *p* is the consideration of grounds for doubt (what Descartes calls *rationes dubitandi*)—hypotheses that we cannot completely rule out but that we view as challenging the belief that *p*, either directly or indirectly. (There is, of course, the possibility that there are hypotheses that would provide us with grounds for doubt but that we have never considered—in which case we would have grounds for doubt without actually having the appropriate doubts.)

If our grounds for doubt are very strong, they may cause us to abandon some of our beliefs. For example, if a juror strongly suspects that the defense's theory of the crime is correct, he or she may cease to believe that the defendant is guilty. Thus, having-doubts-about may lead to doubting-that. Still, having-doubts-about differs from doubting-that: while a person who believes that *p* cannot doubt-that *p*, that person may still have-doubts-about its being the case that *p*—as in the case of the dubious juror.

Calling Beliefs into Doubt

A central claim of *Meditation I* is that Descartes can call each of the beliefs with which he begins the *Meditations* into doubt. Is the claim that, if Descartes believes that *p* at the outset of *Meditations,* he can bring himself to doubt that *p*—or is it simply that, if he believes that *p*, he can produce doubts about its being the case that *p?*

As I've said, Descartes believes that some propositions—such as "2 + 3 = 5"—are so simple and evident that "we can never understand them without believing them to be true" (*Replies II,* AT 7:145). As he himself infers, if a proposition *"p"* is of this sort, we can never doubt that *p*, because doubting-that requires simultaneously understanding a proposition and suspending judgment on its truth. It therefore seems clear that, when Descartes says that "none of [his] beliefs are beyond legitimate doubt," what he has in mind is that each of his beliefs is such that he can have doubts about it. And this in fact is what he indicates when announcing his conclusion: "I'm forced to admit that nothing that I used to believe is beyond legitimate doubt—not because I have been careless or playful, but because I have valid and well-considered grounds for doubt" (AT 7:21). Because these grounds are provided by hypotheses that Descartes himself finds extremely improbable, they fail to produce the suspension of judgment that doubting-that would require, even where such suspense is psychologically possible.

After Descartes arrives at the conclusion that he can call all of his beliefs into doubt—indeed, precisely because he has reached that conclusion—he resolves to "deliberately turn [his] will around, to allow [himself] to be deceived, and to suppose that all [his] previous beliefs are false and illusory" (AT 7:22). Thus, having-doubts-about leads him toward doubting-that. Still, the question posed by the title of *Meditation I*—namely, "Which of the propositions that Descartes believes as he begins the project of the *Meditations* can be called into doubt?"—is a question about having-doubts-about, and the conclusion of *Meditation I*'s main line of argument is simply that, for each proposition *"p,"* if he believes that *p* at the outset of *Meditation I,* he can find grounds for doubt concerning its being the case that *p,* thereby coming to have doubts about its being the case that *p*.

Of course, when finding these grounds for doubt, Descartes does not try to consider his beliefs one by one—an undertaking that he thinks would be "endless" (AT 7:18). Instead, without explicit announcement, he divides his beliefs into two categories, which he considers separately. One category contains what I will call empirical beliefs—beliefs whose justification rests on sensory evidence. (Descartes' examples of beliefs in this category include that he is sitting before a fire, that he is wearing a dressing gown, and that his hands exist [*Med. I,* AT 7:18].) The other category contains what I will call nonempirical beliefs. (His examples of beliefs in this category include that 2 + 3 = 5 and that the square never has more than four sides [*Med. I,* AT 7:20].)

By using the designations *empirical* and *nonempirical,* I have suggested that these categories are exhaustive—a suggestion that Descartes seems to embrace. At the end of *Meditation I,* for example, having argued first that his empirical beliefs and then that his nonempirical are subject to doubt, he concludes, without further ado, that all his beliefs are subject to doubt. But some beliefs do not obviously fall into either category—notably, people's beliefs about their own present experiences. Consider, for instance, my present belief that I am having the sensory experience of seeing brown. If (as I have said) the criterion for a belief's being empirical is that its justification rests on sensory evidence, it's far from clear that my belief that I am seeing brown is empirical. Asked to justify this belief, I might respond that I can offer no empirical evidence (indeed, no evidence of any sort) for it—that I simply know that it is true. On the other hand, my belief that I am now seeing brown does not seem to fit well with the beliefs that I have been calling nonempirical. Although my sensory experiences may not be relevant to the belief's justification, the belief is true precisely because my sensory experiences are as they are, and therefore—unlike Descartes' paradigms of nonempirical beliefs (such as the belief that the square has four sides)—my belief that I am now seeing brown is empirical in some sense of *empirical.* Moreover, while Descartes' paradigmatic examples of nonempirical beliefs concern necessary and eternal truths, the belief that I am now seeing brown concerns a contingent, dated truth. If the belief that I am now seeing brown is in the genus *nonempirical,* it must at least be viewed as importantly different from Descartes' favorite examples of beliefs in that genus.

The position of Pyrrhonian skeptics, with whose works Descartes was familiar,[5] is that we should abandon all our beliefs while continuing to "assent to the appearances." It may be that this position rests on the thought that, although we can of course report (truly or falsely) on our present sensory states, we do not have bona fide beliefs concerning our being in such states. If Descartes accepted some such thought, that acceptance might explain why, when attempting to demonstrate that he can call all of his beliefs in doubt, he never once mentions the beliefs that some later philosophers have regarded as certain beyond question: beliefs about the data of sensation.

Postponing further discussion of this issue, I will grant for the sake of argument that Descartes' categorization of beliefs into empirical and nonempirical is exhaustive. If it is, Descartes can call all of his beliefs by simply producing two hypotheses, one providing grounds for doubt concerning his empirical beliefs and one providing grounds for doubt concerning his nonempirical beliefs.

The Dream Hypothesis

Near the beginning of *Meditation I,* Descartes tries to call all his empirical beliefs into doubt with a single stroke: "I have occasionally caught the senses deceiving me," he writes, "and it's prudent never completely to trust those who have cheated us even once" (AT 7:18).

In evaluating this reasoning, let's limit attention to a single empirical belief—say, Descartes' belief that he is sitting before a fire. The reasoning he offers for our consideration runs, it seems, like this:

When I consider the hypothesis that my senses may be deceiving me now, as I have the experiences that provide me with my only evidence that I am now sitting before a fire, I have some suspicion that it might be true. And, if this hypothesis were true, I would not have any reason for believing that I am sitting before a fire. Accordingly, the thought that my senses are now deceiving me is (for me, now) an unrebutted hypothesis that (indirectly) challenges my belief that I am seated before a fire, and I therefore have doubts about my being before a fire.

The reasoning here is similar to that of the bank clerk described above.

If our sensory apparatuses, like the clerks' machines, are instruments through which we gather evidence for beliefs, the slightest suspicion concerning the reliability of these instruments seems to provide us with (indirect) grounds for doubt concerning beliefs acquired though their use. But Descartes has misgivings about such reasoning. "While my senses may deceive me about what is small is far away," he writes in *Meditation I,* "there may still be other things that I take in by the senses but which I cannot possibly doubt—like that I am here, sitting before the fire" (AT 7:18). If, on a given occasion, there were reliable signs indicating that our senses were not deceiving us, we would sometimes make a mistake by moving from "My senses sometimes deceive me" to "My senses might be deceiving me now."

To answer this objection, Descartes considers the hypothesis that he might be dreaming:

How often, at night, I've been convinced that I was here, sitting before the fire, wearing my dressing gown, when in fact I was undressed and between the covers of my bed! But now I am looking at this piece of paper with my eyes wide open; the head that I am shaking has not been lulled to sleep. . . . None of this would be as distinct if I were asleep. As if I can't remember having been tricked by similar thoughts while asleep! (AT 7:19)

Unable (at the moment) to find any "reliable signs by which [we] can distinguish sleeping from waking," Descartes concludes that he has grounds for doubt concerning each of his particular empirical beliefs, including that he is now sitting before a fire.

The discussion of dreaming also serves another, equally important purpose. While Descartes wants to call particular empirical beliefs into doubt, he also wants to call into doubt broad-ranging empirical beliefs—including the belief that there is a physical world. Though empirical, such general beliefs seem to be confirmed by most occasions on which we have sensory experiences. So, apparently, the only hypothesis that might provide him with grounds for doubt concerning them is that he has been dreaming throughout his entire life—that he is a disembodied mind whose sensory experiences have all been illusory. For convenience, I will call this the dream hypothesis.

Some critics of the *Meditations* argue that, when we say that certain experiences came to us in a dream, we imply (in the strongest sense of that term) that these experiences are inconsistent with others, which we take to be veridical. It follows, according to these critics, that the dream hypothesis is incoherent, and hence that we cannot even suspect that it might be true. But is this really an objection to Descartes' position? By the end of the *Meditations,* Descartes himself has constructed an a priori refutation of the dream hypothesis, showing that it is incoherent in some sense of that term. And why assume that, if a hypothesis is incoherent, we can't suspect that it might be true? It is a necessary, demonstrable truth that the interior angles of a Euclidean triangle sum to exactly two right angles, and the hypothesis that they sum to less is therefore necessarily false—yet beginning students of geometry can, and often do, entertain it. Similarly, Descartes can admit that the dream hypothesis is philosophically incoherent and still say that he suspected that it might be true. In *Meditation I,* he does not claim philosophical clarity, since he is (or, rather, is pretending to be) a philosophical neophyte. And the fact that a philosophical hypothesis is incoherent is not, in itself, an insurmountable obstacle to the neophyte's suspecting that it might be true.

To some extent, we can understand the hypothesis that we might always be dreaming—that all of our experiences are hallucinatory—and we see that, if we were to accept this hypothesis, we wouldn't have any warrant for believing that the physical world exists. To show that we have grounds for doubt concerning empirical proposition, nothing else is required. If critics say that they can prove the hypothesis to be incoherent and thereby rescue many beliefs from the doubts of *Meditation I,* Descartes might reply that that is exactly what he himself intends to do as the *Meditations* progress.

It therefore seems to me that Descartes' argument to the conclusion that he has doubts about each of his empirical beliefs is sound. The consideration of the dream hypothesis provides him with some (very slight) grounds for doubts concerning his belief that he is sitting before a fire, and we can generalize by repeating the argument *mutatis mutandis* for other empirical beliefs.

Belief, the Understanding, and the Will

Having examined Descartes' grounds for doubt concerning his empirical beliefs, I will now turn to beliefs that do not rest on sensory evidence, such as that 2 + 3 = 5. Concerning these beliefs, the dream hypothesis does not seem to provide any grounds for doubt. "Whether we are awake or asleep," Descartes writes, "two plus three is always five, and the square never has more than four sides" (AT 7:20). So the project requires the introduction of a hypothesis of another sort.

Descartes' statement of this new hypothesis rests on a philosophical theory of mental processes—a plausible (if ultimately unacceptable) picture that he does not explicitly explain in the *Meditations*. Since grasping this picture is crucial to understanding Descartes' project, I will sketch it here.

The central thought of the picture is that the human mind has two components—the Understanding and the Will. On this theory, once a person's Understanding grasps a proposition, the person's Will may affirm it, deny it, or do neither.

According to Descartes, if a person's Understanding grasps a proposition *"p"* and the person's Will affirms that proposition, that person believes that *p;* a person whose Will affirms, say, that there are physical objects takes it to be true that there are such objects and, hence, believes that there are. And it seems to me that Descartes would say something stronger. Viewing believing as closely connected to willing, he would say, I suggest, that a person believes that *p* if and *only if* the person's Understanding grasps the proposition *"p"* and the person's Will affirms that proposition.

Some object to this suggestion. While a person must consciously consider the proposition *"p"* for that person's Understanding to grasp that proposition (they argue), people can believe that *p* when they are not consciously considering the proposition *"p."* So, for example, even when all my thoughts are directed elsewhere—indeed, even when I am in dreamless sleep having no thoughts at all—I can be said to believe that the *Meditations* were published in 1641. (Descartes himself seems aware of this point. For instance, when he compares renouncing his beliefs [*opiniones*] to dumping all the apples out of a barrel [*Replies VII*, AT

7:481], he seems to be talking about all the propositions that we would say he believes, not just about those that he has in mind at the moment.) We can therefore distinguish the occurent belief that *p*—which one holds while one is thinking about its being the case that *p*—from the nonoccurent belief that *p*—which one holds at other times. While Descartes' views on the Understanding and the Will may provide a plausible picture of occurent belief (the objection concludes), they do not seem to apply to beliefs of the other sort, and they therefore do not provide us with a complete theory of belief.

But this objection rests on the assumption that, when Descartes says that a person's Understanding grasps a proposition at time *t*, he implies that the person consciously considers that proposition at *t*. To see that this assumption is questionable, consider a typical case of belief: As I look at the rug beneath my feet, I straightforwardly and spontaneously acquire the belief that it is red. I do not ponder the proposition that the rug is red or deliberate about its acceptance, and it would therefore be inappropriate to say that I am considering the proposition "The rug is red." I'm not introspectively viewing any propositions at all; all my attention is directed to the rug. Yet this is a case of belief of exactly the sort that Descartes wants his theory about the Understanding and the Will to explain. So for one's Understanding to grasp a proposition, it may not be necessary that one's awareness be focused on that proposition. To say that my Understanding grasps the proposition that the rug is red may be to say no more than that I understand what it would be like for the rug to be red, where *understand* is used in its usual sense—a sense in which, say, it may be true that a person understands a city's parking regulations even when he or she isn't thinking about them.[6]

Now, on Descartes' theory, the Understanding and the Will generally act independently in the formation of beliefs: the Understanding sometimes comprehends propositions without the Will's either affirming or denying them (as when a person understands the proposition "There is life on planets other than earth" but suspends judgment for lack of evidence), and the Will sometimes affirms or denies propositions that are not well comprehended by the Understanding (as when a person who has only a vague understanding of physics asserts that $E = mc^2$). Still, Descartes contends that as a consequence of the design of our minds, our Understandings sometimes compel our Wills to affirm propositions. Such compulsion, he thinks, is irresistible; when it occurs, we can't do anything to prevent the Will's saying "Yes."

If one person says that 2 + 3 = 5 and a second disagrees, we would naturally infer that the second, if sincere, had misunderstood what the first had said. Descartes' theory suggests a justification (though perhaps not a correct one) for this attitude: if the second person had understood the proposition in question, his Understanding would have compelled his Will to affirm it—assuming (as Descartes does) that the design of the mind responsible for mental compulsion does not differ from one person to another.

According to Descartes, the propositions that our Understandings compel our Wills to affirm fall into two groups. There are, he says, "simple and evident propositions" such as that 2 + 3 = 5, which our Understandings compel our Wills to affirm whenever we consider them (AT 7:21). And there are more complex propositions, which our Understandings compel our Wills to affirm only when certain circumstances obtain. One of Descartes' favorite examples of a proposition of the second sort is that the interior angles of a (Euclidean) triangle sum to two right angles. He writes in *Meditation V,* for instance, "When I consider the nature of the triangle, it seems plain to me—steeped as I am in the principles of geometry—that its three angles equal two right angles: I can't fail to believe this as long as I pay attention to its demonstration" (AT 7:69). While beginning students of geometry may understand the proposition that the internal angles of any triangle sum to two right angles without seeing that the proposition is true, they may find themselves unable to withhold assent after they have mastered the proposition's proof. In idiomatic English, we would call the proof compelling, meaning (Descartes would say) that, when we grasp the proof, our Understandings compel our Wills to affirm its conclusion.

Advances in logical theory, it may seem, have given us a deeper, more satisfying picture of how arguments persuade. If we believe that an argument's premises are true and see that its reasoning is valid, say modern logic texts, we come to see that its conclusion must also be true. Undeniably right—but does it help us to understand how arguments persuade? Consider, for instance, a person who looks at Euclid's proof that the interior angles of a triangle sum to two right angles. Imagine that this person hasn't mastered the use of the terms *angle* and *triangle* and that he or she therefore does not know what the proof's premises mean. Such a person might still believe that these premises are true (because, say, a respected mathematician has sworn a solemn oath on the matter), might believe that the proof is valid (since validity is often a matter of form rather than content), and so might come to believe that the sentence "The internal angles of any Euclidean triangle sum to two right angles" is true. But, in coming to believe this, the person would not necessarily come to believe that the interior angles of all triangles sum to two right angles. So while the textbook explanation of how Euclid's argument persuades may account for how we come to believe that the sentence "The interior angles of all triangles sum to two right angles" is true, it leaves an important question unanswered: How does the proof convince us that the angles of a triangle equal two right angles?

To answer, we might consider the following argument:

If the proposition "The interior angles of a triangle equal two right angles" is true, then the interior angles of a triangle do equal two right angles. The proposition "The interior angles of a triangle equal two right angles" is true. Therefore, the interior angles of a triangle equal two right angles.

By connecting the observation that a certain proposition is true to a geometric fact, this argument may seem to complete the explanation. We see that a proof's premises are true, that its reasoning is valid, and therefore that its conclusion ("The angles of a triangle equal two right angles") must be true—and we then move by the above reasoning to the conclusion that the angles of a triangle equal two right angles. But this explanation falls short in exactly the same way as the first. What was to be explained was how an argument of a certain sort—namely, a geometric proof—convinces us that the interior angles of a triangle equal two right angles. It can hardly help to note that, having completed the proof, we can construct another argument whose conclusion is exactly the same as the proof's. If we found it puzzling that the proof convinces us that the angles of a triangle equal two right angles, we will find it no less puzzling that this other argument does so.

While Descartes' naïve theory of mind may ultimately be unacceptable, it does at least provide us with a plausible picture of how we acquire "intuitively obvious" beliefs (such as that 2 + 3 = 5) and "demonstratively obvious" beliefs (such as that the interior angles of a Euclidean triangle sum to two right angles): as a consequence of the design of our minds, our Understandings sometimes compel our Wills to affirm propositions, thereby producing belief.[7]

If our Understandings compel our Wills to affirm a proposition "*p*," what happens when we consider the negation of "*p*"—or some other proposition that seems to us incompatible with its being the case that *p*? What, for instance, about the propositions "2 + 3 ≠ 5" and "2 + 3 = 6"? To my knowledge, Descartes never explicitly addresses this issue, but we can guess what his position would be. Since he believes that our Wills are compelled to assent to the proposition "2 + 3 = 5" whenever it comes before our Understandings, he probably also believes that our Wills are compelled to deny propositions, such as "2 + 3 ≠ 5," that are plainly inconsistent with "2 + 3 = 5." More generally, it seems likely that, according to Descartes, if a person's Understanding compels his or her Will to affirm that *p* (at time *t*), then (at *t*) that person's Understanding compels his or her Will to deny any proposition that seems to the person to be patently inconsistent with its being the case that *p*.

Such forced denial would differ from the denial of propositions whose falsity is established empirically. In denying, for example, that the paper before me is blue, I might say, "I know what the world would need to be like for the paper to be blue, but I don't believe that the world happens to be that way." In contrast, I do not have any idea what it would be like for two plus three to be more than five. There may be a sense of "understand" in which I can be said to understand this proposition. (Indeed, it might be argued that it is precisely because I do understand it that I know it to be false.) Still, I cannot imagine or suppose or feign that two plus three is more or less than five. While I understand this proposition (in some sense of *understand*), I do not know what it would be like for them to be true.

The Hypothesis of the Evil Demon

In a passage to which I have pointed several times, Descartes says that when our Understandings compel our Wills to affirm a proposition "*p*," we are unable to doubt that *p:*

[Some] perceptions are so evident and at the same time so simple that we cannot ever think of them without believing them to be true. The fact that I exist as long as I am thinking, or that what is done cannot be undone are examples of truths in respect of which we manifestly possess this kind of certainty. For we cannot doubt them unless we think of them, but we cannot think of them without at the same time believing that they are true. . . . There are other truths that are perceived very clearly by our Understandings as long as we attend to the arguments on which our knowledge of them depends, and we therefore are incapable of doubting them during this time. (*Replies II,* AT 7:145)

The reasoning here seems straightforward: For a person to doubt that *p*, he or she must think about its being the case that *p* while not believing that *p*. But, in the case of some propositions, thinking compels believing. So in the case of these propositions, doubting-that is impossible.

Still, Descartes contends that he can have doubts concerning all his beliefs—including those that he cannot prevent himself from holding. Immediately after drawing our attention to several simple and evident propositions (including "2 + 3 = 5" and "The square never has more than four sides") in *Meditation I,* he tells us that "nothing that [he] used to believe is beyond legitimate doubt . . . because [he has] valid and well-considered grounds for doubt" (AT 7:21). To produce grounds for doubt concerning propositions like "2 + 3 = 5," he must find a hypothesis that is unrebutted (for him, in *Meditation I*) and show that this hypothesis somehow challenges his nonempirical beliefs.

Plainly stated, the hypothesis Descartes produces is this:

Descartes' mind is so poorly designed that his Understanding compels his Will to affirm propositions only if those propositions are in fact false.

In *Meditation I,* he makes this hypothesis seem reasonable by associating it with the thought that "there is an evil demon, supremely powerful and cunning, who works as hard as he can to deceive [him]" (AT 7:22). While he firmly believes that there is no such demon, he cannot (at this point) conclusively rule out that there is—and he therefore comes to have some slight suspicion that the connection of his Understanding to his Will might be poorly designed.

But does the hypothesis of the evil demon challenge Descartes' nonempirical beliefs in the way that it must if it is to provide grounds for doubt? This is a difficult question (partly because the idea of challenging is somewhat obscure), but its answer is crucial to the assessment of Descartes' claim that he can call all his beliefs into doubt.

At first glance, it might seem that the hypothesis of the evil demon challenges nonempirical beliefs directly. When Descartes considers, say, his belief that 2 + 3 = 5, can't he reason like this?

That two plus three is five seems so obviously true to me that I cannot prevent myself from believing that two plus three does equal five. In other words, the proposition that two plus three is five is one that my Understanding compels my Will to affirm. But, according to the hypothesis of the evil demon, every proposition that my Understanding compels my Will to affirm is in fact false. So, if this hypothesis were true, it would follow that two plus two does not equal five.

Apparently, if Descartes reasoned this way, he would have grounds for doubt concerning his belief that 2 + 3 = 5: the hypothesis of the evil demon would be unrebutted (for him, in *Meditation I*), and he would see that it directly challenges his belief that 2 + 3 = 5.

But there is a problem here. Earlier, I contended that a hypothesis's incoherence does not necessarily preclude our suspecting that it might be true. But can Descartes really suspect that two plus three might not equal five? To have this suspicion, he would need to be able to have some conception of what it would be like for two plus three to be more or less than five—but, as he tells us, the proposition that 2 + 3 = 5 seems so simple and evident to him that he cannot have such a conception. Indeed, as I suggested earlier, on Descartes' theory, the proposition "Two plus three is more or less than five," being inconsistent with something that his Understanding compels his Will to affirm, is one that he cannot even feign to be true.

And there is another, equally serious problem: If Descartes has any reasons for thinking that the hypothesis of the evil demon directly challenges his belief that 2 + 3 = 5, it is because he has observed that one of the following sentences must be false:

My mind is so poorly designed that whatever seems obviously true to me is false.

It seems obviously true to me that 2 + 3 = 5.

2 + 3 = 5.

But, rather than taking this observation to establish that the hypothesis of the evil demon directly challenges his belief that 2 + 3 = 5, Descartes might take it to refute that hypothesis. "The hypothesis of the evil demon—together with the truth that it seems obvious to me that two plus three is five—entails the absurdity that two plus three does not equal five," he might reason, "and there therefore is no evil demon who deceives me." (An advocate of the hypothesis of the evil demon could not object that the premises of the refutation are dubious, since what is at issue here is whether Descartes' nonempirical beliefs *are* dubious.)

Then might the hypothesis of the evil demon challenges Descartes' belief that 2 + 3 = 5 indirectly? Again, it may seem that the answer is "Yes." Resting on a theory of the relation of the Understanding to the Will, the hypothesis invites us to join skeptics in viewing our minds as instruments for the detection of truth. Apparently, if we suspect that these instruments might be unreliable, that suspicion calls into doubt nonempirical beliefs that arise from their operation.

Compare the case at hand to that of the bank clerk described above. When the clerk places a bill into his machine, it responds (let's suppose) in one of three ways: a green light goes on to indicate that the bill is genuine, a red light goes on to indicate that the bill is counterfeit, or no light goes on. Similarly, when a proposition comes before Descartes' Understanding, there are three possibilities: his Will is compelled to affirm that proposition, his Will is compelled to deny that proposition, or his Will is not compelled to do anything. Just as the clerk notices one day that he cannot fully justify his belief that the machine is reliable, Descartes notices in *Meditation I* that he cannot conclusively rule out the hypothesis of the evil demon—the hypothesis that his mind is a systematically unreliable instrument for the detection of truth. But the clerk's suspicions about his machine provide him with grounds for doubt concerning his belief that the last bill he put through the machine was counterfeit. Then don't Descartes' suspicions about the reliability of his mind as an instrument for the detection of truth provide him with grounds for doubt concerning such beliefs as that 2 + 3 = 5?

Strictly speaking, no. From the fact that the red light goes on when the clerk puts a certain bill through the machine, the clerk infers, and thus comes to believe, that a certain bill is counterfeit. So the hypothesis that the machine is poorly designed indirectly challenges this belief: if the clerk were to accept the hypothesis as true, he would no longer have grounds for holding that belief. In contrast, even on Descartes' own theory, we do not infer that 2 + 3 = 5. That our Undertstandings compel our Wills to affirm that 2 + 3 = 5 does not provide us with evidence for this arithmetic proposition, and it does not lead to our believing that 2 + 3 = 5. On his theory, our Wills' being compelled *is* our believing.

So while the hypothesis of the evil demon does not challenge Descartes' nonempirical beliefs directly, it does not seem to challenge them indirectly either. It cannot undercut Descartes' evidence for simple and evident propositions, since he seems to have—and to need—no evidence for such beliefs.

Still, the hypothesis of the evil demon does somehow seem to challenge Descartes' belief that 2 + 3 = 5. Together with the observation that the proposition "2 + 3 = 5" seems obviously true to him, the hypothesis of the evil demon entails (according to Descartes) that this proposition "appears false to God or to an angel" and is therefore "absolutely speaking, false" (*Replies II*, AT 7:145). Being unable to imagine what it would be like for two plus three to be more or less than five, Descartes may not be able sincerely to say "I suspect that two plus three does not equal five"— but at this point in the *Meditations* nothing prevents him from saying, "I suspect that a certain proposition (namely, '2 + 3 = 5') may be false." That is, while he may not be able to have object-level doubts concerning simple and evident truths, he can have doubts on the meta level. Following Descartes, we might say that these doubts are metaphysical, rather than direct or indirect (AT 7:36).

But the view that the hypothesis of the evil demon grounds metaphysical doubts concerning Descartes' nonempirical beliefs faces a familiar problem: The thought that the proposition "2 + 3 = 5" is false, though not strictly equivalent to the claim that $2 + 3 \neq 5$, does seem to entail it. So the view that the hypothesis of the evil demon challenges Descartes' nonempirical beliefs may seem open to the objection that I raised to the view that this hypothesis challenges his beliefs directly. That is, it may seem that Descartes can refute the hypothesis of the evil demon like this:

My Understanding compels my Will to affirm the proposition "$2 + 3 = 5$." So, if all the propositions that my Understanding compels my Will to affirm were false, the proposition "$2 + 3 = 5$" would be false—and, hence, two plus three would not equal five. But, obviously, two plus three does equal five. So, it's not the case that all the propositions that my Understanding compels my Will to affirm are false.

Why doesn't Descartes offer this reasoning, disprove the hypothesis of the evil demon once and for all, and short-circuit the reasoning of the *Meditations* before it enters the theological labyrinth of *Meditation III?*

The answer, I suggest, is that, in stepping back and reflecting on the workings of his mind, Descartes in effect splits himself in two, erecting a barrier between Descartes as reflector and Descartes as object of reflection. Neither of these "people" can assert all the reasoning's premises. Its first premise—namely, "My Understanding compels my Will to affirm the proposition '$2 + 3 = 5$'"—which seems obviously true to Descartes as reflector, is not something that Descartes as object of reflection accepts, since he does not have philosophical distance on the process through which he has acquired his beliefs. Another premise—namely, "Two plus three does equal five"—which seems obvious to Descartes as object of reflection, would not be accepted by Descartes as reflector, who does not hold object-level arithmetic beliefs. So to refute the hypothesis of the evil demon in the way that I have described, Descartes would need to cross the barrier separating Descartes as reflector from Descartes as object of reflection.

But isn't the barrier contrived? "If Descartes wants to erect this barrier in himself," a reader of the *Meditations* might say, "he's free to do so. But why should I follow him in this?" It seems to me that Descartes has an answer: Each of us clearly can step back and view him- or herself as if viewing another. So while there may seem to be something artificial in my distinction of Descartes as reflector from Descartes as object of reflection, it seems natural for Descartes to write in *Meditation I,* "I think that other people sometimes err in what they believe themselves to know perfectly well. Mightn't I be deceived when I add two and three, or count the sides of a square, or do even simpler things, if we can even suppose that there is anything simpler?" (AT 7:21). If we know about ourselves that our most firmly held beliefs arise in us as the result of psychological processes but we cannot conclusively demonstrate that these processes always lead us to the truth, we must have some misgivings about the truth of each of our most firmly held beliefs—even if, in the case of some of those beliefs, we can't even imagine what it would be like for them to be false.

Accordingly, near the beginning of *Meditation III,* Descartes writes,

When I turn to the things that I believe myself to grasp very clearly, I'm so convinced by them that I spontaneously burst forth saying, "Whoever may deceive me, he will never bring it about that . . . two plus three is either more or less than five, or that something else in which I recognize an obvious inconsistency is true." Since I have no reason for thinking that God is a deceiver—indeed, since I don't yet know whether God exists—the grounds for doubt that rest on the supposition that God deceives are very weak and "metaphysical." Still, to rid myself of these grounds, I ought to ask as soon as possible whether there is a God and, if so, whether He can be a deceiver. For it seems that, until I know these two things, I can never be completely certain of anything else. (AT 7:36)

Descartes' claim here is neither that the hypothesis of the evil demon is incompatible with his belief that 2 + 3 = 5 nor that, if he accepted this hypothesis, he would be deprived of his justification for holding that belief. The hypothesis of the evil demon does not challenge that belief either directly or indirectly. Still, since (at this point in the project) Descartes as reflector cannot conclusively rule out that hypothesis, he has some slight suspicion that some, or perhaps all, the propositions that his Understanding compels his Will to affirm might be false. And, as he sees it, this suspicion provides him with (metaphysical) grounds for doubt concerning the propositions that his Understanding compels his Will to affirm.

A Final Assessment

Has Descartes succeeded in demonstrating that nothing he used to believe is beyond legitimate doubt?

There is the problem (mentioned above) that, although Descartes says nothing to refute the view that we have beliefs about our present sensory experience, he says nothing to call such beliefs into doubt. But, if he hasn't succeeded in calling all his beliefs into doubt, he has at least revealed grounds for doubt concerning many of them. The dream hypothesis provides him with legitimate grounds for doubt concerning his empirical beliefs, since he has some (slight) suspicion that it might be true and sees that it challenges each of these beliefs. Similarly, the hypothesis of the evil demon provides him with grounds for doubt (of a somewhat different nature) concerning his nonempirical beliefs, since he has some slight suspicion that it might be true and sees that, if it were true, the psychological processes through which he acquired his nonempirical beliefs would be systematically unreliable. While the psychological theory underlying his exposition of his position may be unacceptable, there is, as far as I can see, nothing wrong with his conclusion that he has called both his empirical and nonempirical beliefs into doubt.

Resistance to this conclusion arises, in part, from an overestimation of its consequences. It may seem that those who accept it commit themselves to the absurd view that they are not justified in believing, say, that they have hands or that $2 + 3 = 5$. Or it may seem that those who accept this conclusion would be irrational to continue to use their beliefs as guides to action. Or it may seem that those who accept it commit themselves to Descartes' project of supposing all their previous beliefs to be "false and illusory" (AT 7:22)—the project of "overthrowing" their beliefs (AT 7:18), "tearing down everything," and "beginning anew from the foundations" (AT 7:17).

The fact is, however, that acceptance of the conclusion that we have doubts about both our empirical and nonempirical beliefs does not in itself have any of these consequences. As Descartes writes *Meditation I*, he takes himself to have good reason for saying that he is sitting before a fire, he believes that he is sitting before a fire, and he thinks that it is rational both to hold that belief and to act on it. That the dream hypothesis provides him with some minuscule doubts concerning his belief does not change any of that. Thus, near the end of *Meditation I,* after laboring to produce doubts, he says that many of his beliefs are "probable, things that I have much more reason to believe than to deny" (AT 7:22). And this is exactly what he should say. I believe that the floor in my office will bear my weight, preventing me from falling through to the floor below— and I believe that I have very good evidence for that belief. There is no reason for saying that, in itself, the minuscule doubt raised by the dream hypothesis commits me to abandoning that belief or to refusing to act on it. True, in the *Meditations,* Descartes decides to overthrow every belief concerning which he has even the slightest grounds for doubt, and he urges his readers to do the same. But nothing in the demonstration that he has these grounds for doubt forces him (or us) to make this decision.

But, if we accept Descartes' conclusion that we have grounds for doubt concerning our empirical and nonempirical beliefs, doesn't that commit us to the seemingly absurd view that we are not certain of any-thing—the view, for instance, that none of us is certain of his or her own name? Again, I think not. But my reasons for saying so will not emerge until the next chapter, where I will turn from the concept of doubt to the concept of certainty.

CHAPTER 2

Certainty and Stability

Descartes begins *Meditation II* with one of the few emotionally moving images in the *Meditations:*

Yesterday's meditation has hurled me into doubts so great that I can neither ignore them nor think my way out of them. I am in turmoil, as if I have accidentally fallen into a whirlpool and can neither touch the bottom nor swim to the safety of the surface. I will struggle, however. . . . I will continue until I find something certain—or at least I know for certain that nothing is certain. (AT 7:23–24)

Clearly, Descartes was someone who valued certainty very highly—so highly, in fact, that he was willing to risk intellectual drowning to attain it.

Why? The answer for which I will argue in this chapter is that he strove for certainty, not as an end in itself, but as a means to stability of belief. To show this, I will consider what it is to be certain, examine the connection of perfect certainty to perfect stability, and offer a guess as to why Descartes thought his readers valued stability so highly that they would undertake the quest for perfect certainty despite its costs and risks.

Certainty, Doubt, and Stability

Noting that being certain is somehow the opposite of doubting, we might try to define *is certain* like this: To say that person *A* is certain that *p* is to say that *A* does not doubt that *p*. But this would clearly be unacceptable. Since a person who believes that not-*p* does not doubt that *p*, the proposed definition would have the absurd consequence that we are certain of everything we believe to be false. Similarly, since a person who believes that *p* does not doubt that *p*, the proposed definition would entail that we are certain of everything we believe to be true—a consequence that conflicts with our ordinary ways of speaking. Using the term *certain* in its usual sense, we say that we are certain of some of the things we believe but uncertain of others. Indeed, the main use of the term *certain* in ordinary discourse is to mark this distinction.

The moral to be drawn from the failure of the proposed definition is, I suggest, that being-certain-that is not the opposite of doubting-that, but of having-doubts-about. Roughly speaking, to say that a person *A* is certain that *p* is just to say that *A* believes that *p* and has no doubts about its being the case that *p*. This definition of *certain* accords with what is found in many dictionaries, which define *certain* as "having no doubts about."

But, even here, things are not as simple as they might seem. When I consider the hypothesis that everything I have heard about George Washington has been wrong, I judge the probability of this hypothesis being true to be very near zero. Still, I cannot rule it out completely—and I see that, if I were to come to accept it, I would be driven to the conclusion that Washington was not the first president of the United States. Accordingly, the hypothesis directly challenges my belief that Washington was the first president, and I have some doubts about his being the first president. Still, for all that, I would say that I am certain—very certain, though perhaps not perfectly certain—that he was. In this case, as in many others, the doubts are simply too slight to preclude certainty. (Indeed, if certainty were not compatible with some degree of doubt, it would be hard to account for the common practice of saying of two people, both of whom are certain that *p*, that one is more certain than the other.) Accordingly, if our aim is accurately to record current usage, we should perhaps have defined *certain* as "having no *substantial* doubts."

And there is another problem, more important for understanding Descartes' aims in the *Meditations* but less easily solved. As I mentioned earlier, the term *doubt* derives from a Latin verb meaning "to waiver or vacillate." The opposed term *certain* derives from the Latin verb *cernere,* which means "to be stable, secure, or fixed." So to say that a person is certain of something is to imply, if not straightforwardly to say, that it would be difficult to change that person's mind on the matter. There are cases, however, in which a person who has no doubts about a belief can easily be brought to abandon that belief. In such cases, the fact that the person had no doubts inclines us toward saying that he or she was certain, while the fact that the person's belief was unstable inclines us toward saying that he or she was not.

Consider, for example, the following (true) story: Knowing that the library's copy of Descartes' *Principles* does not circulate and that the library has a tight security system, Stewart sincerely announces that he is certain that the book is in the library. But then someone reminds him of something he knew but had forgotten: because the library is being painted, most of its books have temporarily been moved to another building. Immediately on being reminded of this, Stewart comes to have doubts about the book's being in the library—doubts so strong that he ceases even to believe that the book is there. The ground for these doubts is of course the hypothesis that the book in question was among those moved.

Before being reminded of the renovation, was Stewart certain? If being certain simply amounts to having no substantial doubts, he was—as he himself sincerely announced. Yet there is an oddity to saying so. Since he already knew that books had been moved out of the library, he had grounds for doubt concerning his belief that the book was there, even though momentarily, because of a lapse of memory, he was unaware of those grounds. Although the English term *certain* derives from a Latin term having to do with being fixed and stable, his belief was unstable and easily overthrown.

While the instability of Stewart's belief may not preclude our saying that he was certain, it does show that there are two components to the ordinary idea of certainty. The concept of certainty is connected on the one hand to the concept of lacking substantial doubts, and on the other hand to the concept of stability. In some cases (like the one I have described), these two components seem to clash.

In other cases, of course, the components fit happily together. Suppose, for example, that a person who believes something lists the most obvious and most probable hypotheses that might challenge his or her belief and then somehow conclusively rules each of them out. To shake this person of his or her belief, we would need to rely on the concealed or improbable. Accordingly, in ruling out substantial doubts about a belief, a person tends to stabilize that belief—to immunize it to challenge. So, while the ordinary conception of certainty contains two components that sometimes pull in opposite directions, those components are connected.

Perfect Certainty

What Descartes seeks in the *Meditations* is not garden-variety certainty of the sort that I examined in the last section, but something that he calls *perfect certainty* [*perfectissima certitudo*]. (See, for example, *Replies II*, AT 7:145.) Certainty of this extreme sort differs from ordinary certainty in two ways.

First, as I pointed out in the last section, we ordinarily say that people are certain even if they have some small doubts—but a person who holds the belief that *p* with perfect certainty would have no doubts at all about its being the case that *p*.

Second, using the term *certain* in the usual way, we may say that people are certain of something when they are not aware of any grounds for doubt concerning that thing, even if they have grounds for doubt that they have forgotten or overlooked. (Accordingly, we might say, concerning the case considered above, that Stewart was certain that the book was in the library even though he could very easily be brought to see that he had grounds for doubt concerning its being there.) But a person who holds the belief that *p* with perfect certainty would have no grounds for doubt at all concerning its being the case that *p*—not even grounds of which he or she was unaware. In short, to say that a person is perfectly certain that *p* is to say that the person has somehow conclusively ruled out every hypothesis that—in any way or to any degree—might challenge the belief that *p*.

It follows that, if a person holds the belief that *p* with perfect certainty, that belief cannot be overthrown. Having conclusively ruled out every hypothesis that might provide grounds for doubt concerning the belief, the person would not experience, hear, observe, or otherwise discover anything that would make it unreasonable to continue to hold that belief. Indeed, having conclusively ruled out all grounds for doubt concerning its being the case that *p*, the person would not discover anything that might even provide grounds for misgivings or reservations about believing that *p*. In other words, if a person had perfect certainty concerning one of his or her beliefs, that belief would be perfectly firm and stable.

The Value of Certainty

At first glance, it may seem obvious that (other things being equal) certainty is desirable. "If I were lost in a desert," one might say, "I would much rather that my guide be certain that there is water to the north than merely have a hunch that there is." But now imagine two guides: *A*, who is certain that there is water to the north, and *B*, who tentatively holds the belief that there is. Both will lead us in the same direction. And, if we examine *A*'s reasons for believing that there is water to the north, mightn't we find that those reasons are bad and that *A* is therefore more certain than the evidence warrants—just as the Aristotelians who refused to look through Galileo's telescope were too certain of their cosmology? In some cases, certainty—far from being something desirable—seems to be an intellectual vice.

And even if certainty is desirable, is perfect certainty so valuable that we ought to pay a high price to achieve it? Think, for instance, about my belief that 2 + 3 = 5. While the hypothesis of the evil demon may provide me with some (very slight) grounds for doubt concerning this belief, and while I therefore may not be perfectly certain, I am still *very* certain. Becoming perfectly certain would require some time and effort—even in the fictional framework of the *Meditations,* five days of seclusion and intense mental labor. Would it be worth the effort? If I'm already very certain that 2 + 3 = 5, would I be any better off being more certain? If so, would the gain be sufficient to justify five days' work, when I have other things to do that might promise more consequential rewards?

Bernard Williams has argued that we should understand Descartes' quest for certainty against the background of his commitment to "the project of pure enquiry." To undertake this project, Williams explains, is to make a completely uncompromising attempt to raise one "truth ratio" to unity—one's truth ratio being the number of one's true beliefs divided by the total number of one's beliefs. According to Williams, success in this attempt requires that one adopt a method that is both "error proof" and "epistemologically effective"—that is, it must be impossible to acquire a false belief by application of the method, and the inquirer must be able to tell, as he proceeds, whether he is applying the method properly. Believing that a person who adopts such a method will, ipso facto, become certain of each of the beliefs that he or she acquires, Williams concludes that the pure inquirer's search for truth necessarily becomes the search for certainty. "What is needed by the pure enquirer is an error proof method which is epistemologically effective," he writes. "This *comes to* the requirement that the beliefs which the method generates be certain."[1] Thus, according to Williams, since we can understand why a philosopher like Descartes might undertake the project of pure enquiry, we can understand why such a philosopher would take up the quest for certainty.

But is it necessarily the case that beliefs acquired through an error proof and epistemologically effective method are certain? One might apply such a method and be highly dubious of the results because one didn't believe that the method was error proof. More to the point, even if one were firmly convinced that one's method was error proof, one might still be dubious of the results of that method's application if one had in mind grounds for doubt concerning the method's reliability.

As I see it, this is Descartes' epistemic state at the end of *Meditation I*. Although he firmly believes that, say, the methods of mathematics never lead to falsehood, and although he can tell as he goes along whether he is applying those methods correctly, the hypothesis of the evil demon provides him with some (very slight) doubts concerning propositions like "2 + 3 = 5," and he therefore is not perfectly certain of their truth. It therefore seems to me a mistake to think that we can explain Descartes' seeking perfect certainty simply by noting that he is engaged in "the project of pure enquiry."

Janet Broughton suggests another explanation for Descartes' striving for certainty—namely, that by doing so, he may be able to "dislodge us from our ordinary beliefs."[2] To illustrate, Broughton asks us to suppose that she has two beliefs—the belief that *p* and the belief that *q*—both of which are "completely free from the everyday worries we may have about our beliefs." She also asks us to suppose that, although she can find "no grounds whatsoever for being less than entirely certain about *p*," she does have some slight grounds for doubt concerning *q*. Finally, she asks us to suppose "that *p* and *q* conflict"—that is, that they cannot both be true. According to Broughton, it is plausible that, in a case of this sort, we ought to believe that *p* and disbelieve that *q*. "I ought to believe what I am absolutely certain about," she writes, "and disbelieve whatever conflicts with those absolute certainties, even if that means disbelieving something about which I am morally certain." So, in Broughton's view, Descartes' resolution to accept only what is perfectly certain provides him with a way to shake people free from firmly held convictions—and, in particular, to dislodge Aristotelianism in preparation for the acceptance of the New Science.

If my analysis of perfect certainty is right, however, Broughton's description of this way is incoherent. Clearly, in the case she describes, we are to assume not only that *p* and *q* are contraries, but that she sees that they are contraries. Otherwise, why would her acceptance of *p* cause her to disbelieve that *q*? And, since at the outset she believes that *q* (indeed, is morally certain that *q*), we can infer that she has not conclusively ruled *q* out. Accordingly, at the outset, she could not have been perfectly certain of *p* after all: being an unrebutted hypothesis that is known to be inconsistent with *p*, *q* itself provides her with grounds for doubt concerning *p*. If Descartes had tried to shake people from their convictions in the way Broughton describes, he could not possibly have succeeded.

We therefore return to the question that I posed earlier: If I am very certain that *p*, what would I gain by becoming perfectly certain that *p*?

In answering these questions from Descartes' point of view, it's important to see that the attainment of perfect certainty is not his primary aim in the *Meditations*. This is clear from the first sentence of *Meditation I:* "For several years now I've been aware that I accepted many falsehoods as true in my youth, that what I built on the foundations of those falsehoods was dubious, and accordingly that once in my life I would need to tear down everything and begin anew from the foundations if I wanted to establish any stable and lasting knowledge" (AT 7:17). As Descartes here indicates, his primary aim in the *Meditations* is to achieve stability in his system of beliefs. He desires certainty—or, more precisely, perfect certainty—as a means to that end.

In Descartes' Latin, the sentence expressing this means-to-end relationship would have the ring of a tautology, since the word used for *certainty* and the one used for *stability* would both derive from the same Latin root: *certus*. And, as I indicated in the last section, this linguistic fact points to a conceptual connection. To attain perfect certainty concerning a given belief, a person would need conclusively to rule out, once and for all, each hypothesis that in any way challenged that belief, removing even the slightest suspicion that it might be true. In doing so, the person would discover and definitively refute everything that might make it unreasonable to continue to hold that belief—indeed, everything that might challenge the belief. Thus, unlike "the many falsehoods that [he] accepted as true in [his] youth," perfectly certain beliefs would be "firm and stable"—completely immune to refutation or challenge.

But, if Descartes desired perfect certainty as a means to stability, why did he desire stability so highly? There may of course be answers that have to do with his personal circumstances or peculiarities of his personality. But, to understand the *Meditations,* we need a more general answer. Although Descartes wrote the *Meditations* autobiographically, he obviously hopes that his readers generally will follow his lead and go through the program themselves. Whatever reason Descartes might give for valuing stability, we should expect it to be one that many of his readers would also accept.

This reason, I suggest, has to do with Descartes' times. In 1593, when Descartes was born, European scientists accepted a picture of the universe derived from Aristotle's works. By the end of the seventeenth century, however, every basic tenet of Aristotelian theory had been challenged and rejected. The trauma of replacing one scientific outlook with another, which would have been great under any circumstances, was magnified by the scope of the change, the militancy of the opposition to it, and the association of scientific change with the aesthetic, economic, religious, and political revolutions of the seventeenth century.[3] Descartes witnessed all but the last steps of this revolutionary change. Indeed, although he seems not to have viewed himself in this way, he was in the forefront of the revolutionaries. Educated as an Aristotelian, he became a principle figure in the New Science. His development of algebraic geometry paved the way for Newton's mathematics, as his identification of the principles of physics with the principles of geometry paved the way for the geometric treatment of matter that characterized the new physics. He was the first major scientist to advocate the principles of rectilinear inertia and conservation of momentum—principles that were to become cornerstones of Newtonian physics. (Newton acknowledged his debts to Descartes by echoing the name of one of Descartes' works, *The Principles of Philosophy*, in the title of his own seminal work, *The Fundamental Principles of Mathematical Philosophy*.)

As a creative scientist, Descartes may have been distressed by the prospect of his own contributions being ridiculed, maligned, and rejected like those of almost all scientists before him. Or, while there is little evidence of social conscience in the *Meditations,* he may have wanted to spare future generations the intellectual, political, and spiritual havoc that he saw follow in the wake of the scientific upheaval of his own day. In any case, that his desire for stability was aroused by the scientific revolution is clear from the *Meditations'* first sentence: "For several years now, I've been aware that I accepted many falsehoods as true in my youth." Descartes wrote this sentence not for readers at a remove of several hundred years, but for those of his own time who could read Latin and understand technical philosophical argument. The members of this elite group surely would have understood the "falsehoods" that he mentions to include all the basic tenets of what had passed for scientific knowledge just a short time before. Such readers would not have wondered, as recent readers sometimes do, what might have driven a scientist of the day to risk intellectual drowning in the quest for knowledge that would be stable and lasting.

Since the method of doubt, which the quest for perfect certainty seems to require, forces people to relinquish their Aristotelian prejudices, Descartes' advocacy of the New Science may have influenced his decision to aim for perfect certainty—even if he himself was unaware of the influence. Still, it seems to me to be a mistake to think that his primary philosophical aim in the *Meditations* was to provide a foundation for the developing sciences. Many of his readers, including some of the authors of the *Objections,* would not have been moved to follow the program of the *Meditations* by the thought that it might clear the way for scientific innovation. (In fact, Aristotelians might have taken that thought as a reason for not engaging in the program.) But almost all of Descartes' readers would have shared his desire for stability—in epistemology and theology as well as in science. If we ask "Why did Descartes search for certainty?" hoping to learn why he expected others (including those who did not share his confidence in the emerging new science) to join him in that search, the answer is that he wanted to avoid, for all time, intellectual turmoil of the sort that plagued Europe during his lifetime.

CHAPTER 3

Method

For reasons outlined in Chapter 1, Descartes thinks that he has grounds for doubt concerning each of the beliefs with which he begins the *Meditations,* that he is not perfectly certain of anything, and that each of his beliefs is therefore such that future circumstances may make it reasonable for him to abandon it. Thinking that no piecemeal strategy will succeed in leading him to perfect certainty, he therefore resolves "to tear down everything and begin anew from the foundations." Nothing in the argument of *Meditation I* forces him (or his readers) to this extraordinary decision; finding that perfect certainty is difficult, if not impossible, to attain, he could reasonably have decided to settle for less. But he has set out on a quest for perfect certainty, and he resolves to persevere.

In *Replies VII*[1] (where Descartes' tone is sometimes petulant) he describes the process of this quest through commonplace analogies. When we suspect that some of the apples in a barrel are rotten, he says, we should empty them all out and replace only those that we have examined thoroughly (AT 7:481). And, if we are building on sandy soil, we should clear the land and dig down to bedrock before starting construction (AT 7:537). Both of these images indicate that the process has two movements: emptying or demolishing, and refilling or rebuilding. In this chapter, I will look at both of these movements.

"Emptying the Barrel"?

What in Descartes' project might correspond to "dumping the apples out of the barrel"?

The obvious answer is that dumping the apples out of the barrel corresponds to his somehow ridding himself of all his beliefs, creating a (temporary) state of belieflessness. But this answer is unacceptable. As I've explained, Descartes holds that there are propositions that his Understanding compels his Will to affirm—nonempirical propositions that he can't prevent himself from believing. If "emptying the barrel" required ceasing to believe these propositions, his own theory of mind would entail that the emptying could not be completely successful.

Even ridding ourselves of empirical beliefs would not be an easy matter, since such beliefs seem not to be within our direct, conscious control. To get the apples out of a barrel, we simply pick the barrel up and turn it over but, when a person sees a desk before him, what can he do to rid himself of the belief that the desk exists? Simply commanding one's self to abandon the belief isn't likely to have any effect whatever.

Partly for these reasons, Harry Frankfurt has suggested that, to empty the barrel, one need not cease to hold one's beliefs. For comparison, Frankfurt asks us to imagine a mathematician who is constructing a system of arithmetic, to suppose that the mathematician has not yet established a certain proposition as a theorem of his system, and to notice that—regardless of what the mathematician believes—he or she quite properly refuses to use this proposition as a premise in proofs. Emptying the barrel, Frankfurt suggests, is like that. "Within the limited context created by his intention to develop a system of knowledge," he writes, Descartes' "resolution to overthrow all his opinions . . . demands no more of him than a recognition that the slate of his proposed theory is clean because he does not yet know any proposition to have a legitimate place in the system of knowledge he wishes to construct."[2]

But there is a problem with Frankfurt's analogy. Even when people construct mathematical systems, rigorously deducing theorems from axioms and previously proven theorems, their beliefs can subtly influence their reasoning. (Euclid himself begins writing about the interior angles of the triangle without having demonstrated that triangles have an in-side and an outside.) In less formal systems, such as the one Descartes constructs in the *Meditations,* the risk is much greater, since some of our premises and rules of inference may not be explicitly laid out for scrutiny. And the risk of our being influenced by unproven beliefs multiplies again when the system in question is not a formal structure that we consider on special occasions, but the entire collection of beliefs on which we base the activities of daily life.

Descartes acknowledges this risk near the end of *Meditation I:*

My habitual views constantly return to my mind and take control of what I believe as if our long-standing, intimate relationship has given them the right to do so, even against my will. I'll never break the habit of trusting and giving in to these views while I see them for what they are—things somewhat dubious (as I have just shown) but nonetheless probable, things that I have much more reason to believe than to deny. (AT 7:22)

When it looks and feels to Descartes that he is sitting before a fire, habits of thought might lead him to affirm that he *is* there—especially if he is inattentive. Similarly, he might reason unreflectively from the observation that a certain figure is a triangle to the conclusion that it has three sides, influenced beneath the level of conscious awareness by his belief that triangles have three sides. Accordingly, to ensure that the propositions of his new system will not be infected by the doubts that he has raised concerning his previous beliefs, he must do more than simply wipe clean his slate of theorems. He must adopt a method that somehow isolates him from the influence of his intellectual habits and inclinations.

Descartes' homey analogy about dumping the apples out of a barrel therefore conceals a dilemma. On the one hand, emptying the barrel does not seem to require ridding ourselves of all our beliefs. On the other hand, it does seem to require more than simply maintaining control of the premises that we use in our arguments. What, then, is it to dump the apples out of the barrel?

Skeptical Counterbalancing and the Demon's Advocate

One way to approach the question of what Descartes means when he writes about emptying the barrel is to examine the process by which he tries to accomplish the emptying.

As has often been noted, that way derives from the skeptical method of tropes.[3] To apply this method to a given belief, skeptics find (or, failing that, imagine) a being that holds an opposed belief. To doubt that the colors they see are those truly in objects, for example, they conjecture that nonhuman animals, which have organs of sight different from theirs, see colors differently. To doubt that the tastes they detect are those truly in foods, they conjecture that other people, whose constitutions differ from theirs, taste things differently. To doubt that a bowl of water has the temperature that it seems to them to have, they note that it might seem to have another temperature to someone whose body is in a different condition. To doubt that a boat that seems small and stationary is so, they note that it might seem large and moving to those closer to it. To call their moral beliefs into doubt, they find people of different cultures who do not share those beliefs.[4]

Having imagined a being with a belief contrary to his or her own, the skeptic asks, "Is there anything I can say to this being to convince it that my belief is right and its belief wrong?" According to the skeptic, the answer is often "No." Even if the other being can understand speech and follow argument, there may be nothing we can say or do that should change that being's mind. (If a sick man stubbornly insists that the sugar that tastes bitter to him is not sweet, for instance, what can we do or say to convince him that he is wrong?) "But, if someone as reasonable as I am can listen to all the evidence and still not be convinced to accept my belief," asks the skeptic, "how can I view myself as having conclusive reason for holding that belief? If I can't convince others, I must not really have knowledge of the matter myself."

In *Rules for the Direction of the Mind*,[5] Descartes offers a similar thought:

When two people arrive at opposite judgments on the same matter, it's certain that one of them is wrong, and it seems that *neither* has knowledge—for, if the reasoning of one were certain and clear, he would be able to lay it before the other in such a way as eventually to convince [the other's] Understanding as well. (AT 10:363)

Descartes does not here advocate the strong skeptical principle that one has no warrant at all for holding a belief unless one can convince others, but he does subscribe to a similar principle: on his view, it's likely that one does not truly know that *p* unless, given the time and the opportunity, one could convince others that *p*.

This thesis is central to the method by which Descartes tries to isolate himself from the beliefs with which he begins the *Meditations*. In the attempt to rid himself of many of his beliefs and to protect himself from the unwanted influence of others, he imagines a person who holds beliefs opposite from his. Then, having imagined this person, he resolves to pretend to be him—to play him in the way that an actor plays a part. When this other person speaks in the *Meditations,* it is of course through Descartes and in the first person—but I will view him as distinct from Descartes and (for reasons that will become obvious) dub him the Demon's Advocate.

Descartes and the Demon's Advocate are very much alike. They have exactly the same sensory experiences, they agree that propositions like "2 + 3 = 5" seem obviously true, and they agree on which arguments are valid. Yet there is an important difference: while Descartes believes his mind to be the product of a benevolent God, the Demon's Advocate believes that "there is an evil demon, supremely powerful and cunning, who works as hard as he can to deceive [him]" (AT 7:22). From this fundamental difference issue two others: (i) While Descartes believes that his senses are generally reliable, the Demon's Advocate believes that his senses are systematically deceptive, and (ii) while Descartes believes that the propositions that seem obviously true to him are true, the Demon's Advocate believes that such propositions are false.

In the early sixteenth century, the Church established the office of the Promotor Fidei—commonly called the Advocatus Diaboli, or Devil's Advocate. When someone was proposed for sainthood, the Devil's Advocate tried to construct the strongest case that he could against the proposal. The idea, it seems, was that the truth would emerge from adversarial proceedings in which a candidate's supporters debated someone who had been assigned the task of arguing in opposition. Similarly, in the *Meditations,* Descartes thinks that certainty will emerge from a discussion in which he debates his own invention, the Demon's Advocate.

Imagine a dialogue between Descartes and the Demon's Advocate on, say, whether there is a desk before them. Descartes might begin like this:

I am having various visual and tactile sensations that make it seem to me that there is now a desk before me. And my senses are generally reliable—especially in situations like these. Therefore, there (probably) is a desk before me.

The Demon's Advocate might reply like this:

I am having exactly the same visual and tactile sensations as Descartes, and these sensations make it seem to me, as to him, that there is a desk before me. But my senses are invariably deceptive. Therefore, it's false that there is a desk before me.

We can imagine a similar dialogue on the truth of nonempirical propositions. Descartes might begin by saying,

It seems so obvious to me that $2 + 3 = 5$ that my belief that $2 + 3 = 5$ requires no justification.

The Demon's Advocate might reply,

The proposition "$2 + 3 = 5$" seems obviously true to me, because my Understanding compels my Will to affirm it. But the connection of my Understanding to my Will has been designed by an evil demon who works as hard as he can to deceive me. So propositions seem obviously true to me only if they are in fact false. Therefore, the propositions that my Understanding compels my Will to affirm—including "$2 + 3 = 5$"—are false.

While the Demon's Advocate may not be able sincerely to assert that two plus three is not five, he can apparently assert of a certain proposition (such as "$2 + 3 = 5$") that it is false—provided that he remains at the meta level of discourse. (See Chapter 1.)

There is a point to regarding Descartes' beliefs and those of the Demon's Advocate as mirror images. Generally, Descartes believes that *p* just in case the Demon's Advocate believes that "*p*" is false.

True, Descartes and the Advocate agree on how things seem. They agree, for example, that it looks as though there is a sun. Since we might view a person who says "It looks to me as though the sun exists" as expressing a belief about his own sensory states, it may seem that the Descartes and the Advocate share beliefs after all. But this is not how Descartes sees it. On his view, I suggest, someone who asserts that it looks to him as though the sun exists isn't indicating that his Will has affirmed the proposition "The sun exists," but only that his Will is inclined toward affirming that proposition. And, if Descartes takes some such line, he can consistently maintain both that he and the Advocate agree on the appearances and that their systems of belief are mirror images.

Besides agreeing on the appearances, Descartes and the Advocate agree on matters of logic and, in particular, on which arguments are valid. If Descartes does not take himself to be able to distinguish valid arguments from invalid arguments, the project of achieving perfect certainty through the application of reason would obviously be doomed from the outset.[6] Similarly, if the fiction of the Demon's Advocate is to serve its function, Descartes must assume that the Advocate is also rational in this way. That Descartes is unable to convince a raving lunatic of the truth of some proposition hardly suggests that "neither of them has knowledge" (to use Descartes' phrase in the *Rules*) or provides him with the "counterbalance" for whose sake the Advocate was called into being. That, I suggest, is why Descartes goes out of his way in *Meditation I* to distinguish his grounds for doubt from those of "madmen whose brains are so rattled by the persistent vapors of melancholy that they are sure that they're kings when in fact they are paupers, or that they wear purple robes when in fact they're naked, or that their heads are clay, or that they are gourds, or made of glass" (AT 7:19).[7] It may seem that the chances of Descartes' settling his disagreements with the Advocate through reasoning are minuscule, but there obviously would be no chance at all if they disagree about what counts as an acceptable argument—either because the Advocate is a lunatic or because the Descartes is.

The difference between Descartes and the Demon's Advocate concerns a matter of fact: Descartes believes that his mind is properly designed, while the Advocate believes that his mind has been systematically misdesigned by an evil demon. The Advocate has very little reason for thinking that there is an evil demon—perhaps no reason at all. Still, since Descartes initially has very little reason for thinking that his mind is a reliable instrument for detecting truth, the Advocate's beliefs are no less reasonable and well founded than Descartes' own. Both systems rest on unconfirmed foundations.

Of course, judged by ordinary standards, the Demon's Advocate is insane; if we ran into him (outside a philosophy classroom) we might suggest psychotherapy or institutionalization. But he is aware of all the evidence available to Descartes, he will listen to argument, and he agrees with Descartes about what reasoning is acceptable. So, at the beginning of the *Meditations,* Descartes must regard the Advocate as just as informed and as rational as he is.

In consequence, the fiction of the Demon's Advocate helps Descartes to isolate himself from his previous beliefs and habits. If he is inclined to assert a proposition or use it in his reasoning, he can pretend to be the Demon's Advocate and so thwart his inclinations. So, for instance, when he is inclined to assert a proposition about a material object, Descartes can say to himself,

I will suppose [*supponam*], . . . not that there is a supremely good God who is the source of all truth, but that there is an evil demon, supremely powerful and cunning, who works as hard as he can to deceive me. I will say that sky, air, earth, color, shape, sound, and other external things are just dreamed illusions that the demon uses to ensnare my judgment. I will regard myself as not having hands, eyes, flesh, blood, and senses—but as having the false belief that I have all these things. (AT 7:22)

Thus, if Descartes' sensory experiences incline him toward saying that there is an earth, the observation that the Demon's Advocate says that the proposition "There is an earth" is false provides him with a way to resist the inclination.

Descartes records this point with a mechanical metaphor:

I think it will be good deliberately to turn my will around, to allow myself to be deceived, and to suppose that all my previous beliefs are false and illusory. Eventually, when I have counterbalanced the weight of my prejudices [*aequatis utrimque praejudicorum ponderibus*], my bad habits will no longer distort my grasp of things. (AT 7:22)

The image here is of scales. Descartes' old beliefs have weight, which draws him toward affirming various propositions, but the fiction of the Demon's Advocate provides him with a counterbalance.

Skepticism Versus Cartesianism

Looking back, scientists of Descartes' day naturally wondered what had gone wrong with Aristotelian science. Without some understanding of where their predecessors had failed, how could they hope to avoid the errors—and, hence, the fate—of the Aristotelians?

One line of thought (familiar, for example, from Locke's *Essay Concerning Human Understanding*) is that Aristotelian scientists had not done anything wrong, except perhaps to overestimate their doctrines' longevity. On this view, nothing scientists can do will ever elevate their results above the level of unstable, plausible conjecture. To support this view, philosophers sometimes used arguments similar to those that Descartes considers at the beginning of *Meditation I*. If we can always use arguments of this sort to show that our beliefs are subject to doubt, perfect certainty—and its correlate perfect stability—must be unattainable.

Descartes' belief, in contrast, was that perfect certainty and stability are within human reach. The problem, as he saw it, was one of method. If scientists before him had followed a proper method, he thought, the science they developed could not have been overthrown.[8]

The method that Descartes himself adopts is closely connected to production of doubt in *Meditation I*. There, what he finds wrong with his beliefs is that the dream hypothesis and the hypothesis of the evil demon call them into doubt. To rescue these propositions from doubt—that is, to become perfectly certain of their truth and so justify his placing them into the new system that he is developing—he must conclusively refute these hypotheses. Since the underlying difference between the Demon's Advocate and Descartes is that the Advocate accepts these hypotheses as true, we can say that, to achieve perfect certainty, Descartes must silence the Demon's Advocate. In the attempt at refutation, however, he cannot appeal to propositions (such as "There is a veracious God") from which he has distanced himself in the process of isolation—which is to say that, in silencing the Demon's Advocate, he cannot appeal to any proposition whose truth the Demon's Advocate denies.

Descartes' task is therefore clear: to achieve perfect certainty, he must conclusively refute both the dream hypothesis and the hypothesis of the evil demon, and he must do so to the satisfaction of the hypotheses' main proponent, the Demon's Advocate. In consequence, his method in *Meditations II, III,* and *IV* centers on a single rule: Accept a proposition "*p*" as perfectly certain and allow it into your new system of beliefs if and only if you believe that *p* and can convince the Demon's Advocate that "*p*" is true.

Descartes' acceptance of this rule is reflected in the *Meditations'* prose. At the moment he establishes the rule, the *Meditations* become a debate between Descartes and the Demon's Advocate. Descartes states a thesis, objects to it in the voice of the Demon's Advocate, replies as himself, answers as the Demon's Advocate, and so on. Consider, for example, this short passage from the beginning of *Meditation II:* "Isn't there a God, or something like one, who puts my thoughts into me? But why should I say so when I may be the author of those thoughts? Well, isn't it at least the case that I am something? But I now am denying that I have senses and a body" (AT 7:24). Here, in the span of about fifty words, Descartes changes voices four times. In the first and third sentences, he speaks as himself and, in the second and fourth, as the Demon's Advocate.

Reflecting on the fundamental differences between Descartes and the Demon's Advocate, we might wonder whether Descartes can convince the Demon's Advocate of anything and, consequently, whether he will ever be able to claim perfect certainty about any of his beliefs. At the outset of *Meditation II,* Descartes wonders about this himself. "I have no senses," he writes (in the voice of the Demon's Advocate). "Body, shape, extension, motion, and place are fantasies. What then is true? Perhaps just that nothing is certain" (AT 7:24). As I will show in the next chapter, however, Descartes does manage to convince the Demon's Advocate of something: his own existence. And, as I will argue in Chapter 6, he also identifies a general strategy by means of which he can convince the Demon's Advocate of much more. If this strategy fails (I will argue) it is because Descartes is unable to complete some of the tactics that it requires—not because every debate between Descartes and the Demon's Advocate must necessarily end in a standoff.

CHAPTER 4

The Riddle of the Cogito

As I have argued, the *Meditations* are the report of a project whose aim is the attainment of perfect certainty and whose method involves Descartes' playing the role of a fictitious person—the Demon's Advocate—who believes that his senses are deceptive and that his mind is poorly designed. Descartes will regard his belief that *p* as perfectly certain only if he can persuade the Demon's Advocate that "*p*" is true.

The first proposition that Descartes places on the list is "I am":

Isn't there a God, or something like one, who puts my thoughts into me? But why should I say so when I may be the author of those thoughts? Well, isn't it at least the case that I am something? But I now am denying that I have senses and a body. But I stop here. For what follows from these denials? Am I so bound to my body and to my senses that I cannot exist without them? I have convinced myself that there is nothing in the world—no sky, no earth, no minds, no bodies. Doesn't it follow that I don't exist? No, surely I must exist if it's me who is convinced of something. But there is a deceiver, supremely powerful and cunning, whose aim is to see that I am always deceived. But surely I exist, if I am deceived. Let him deceive me all he can, he will never make it the case that I am nothing while I think that I am something. Thus having fully weighed every consideration, I must finally conclude that the statement "I am, I exist" must be true whenever I state it or mentally consider it. (*Med. II,* AT 7:25)

The reasoning of this passage is often summarized with the slogan *Cogito ergo sum* ["I think, therefore I am"],[1] and the passage itself is often called the Cogito after this slogan.

While the language of the Cogito is conversational and nontechnical, there has been controversy from Descartes' time onward about how its reasoning runs—and indeed about whether it contains reasoning. In the initial sections of this chapter, I will explore this controversy by looking critically at several common readings of the Cogito: the intuitive interpretation, the inferential interpretation, the performative interpretation, and an interpretation according to which the certainty of "I am" arises out of the doubts of *Meditation I*. Then, drawing on the system of concepts that I developed in Chapter 2, I will offer a fifth reading, which I will call the doubt-dispelling interpretation. Finally, I will look at how the Cogito changes Descartes' conception of himself.

The Cogito as the Report of Intuition

In *Rules for the Direction of the Mind*, Descartes contends that there are two fundamentally different ways to gain nonempirical knowledge: intuition and inference (*Rule III*, AT 10:366–70).

Derived from a Latin verb meaning "to look," the term *intuition* was used in medieval theological writing to name the sense through which angels see what is happening without the use of bodily organs such as eyes. When Descartes uses the term, it retains some of its theological connotations: to intuit, in the Cartesian sense of the term, is to see that something is so by using the mind's eye rather than the bodily senses. Among his examples of propositions whose truth we intuit is "2 + 3 = 5." Asked to explain why we believe that a proposition of this sort is true, we might reasonably say that we do not have any evidence and that none is required—that the truth of such propositions is simply obvious.

On Descartes' theory, demonstrations are aids to intuition. Given the proof, say, of a geometric theorem, we see that the theorem is true in roughly the same way we see that 2 + 3 = 5. The difference is that, while intuition happens all at once, inference may involve a number of acts performed in sequence. To illustrate this difference, Descartes distinguishes two ways of verifying that the first link of a chain is connected to the last. We can see the whole chain and observe the relation of the first link to the last in a single act of vision, or we can see that the first link is connected to the second, the second to the third, the third to the fourth, and so on. According to Descartes, the first of these ways of seeing the chain stands to the second as intuition stands to demonstration (*Rule III,* AT 10:369–70).

While "I am" is not a necessary truth like "2 + 3 = 5," there seems to be a reason for saying that we intuit its truth. Asked why we believe that we exist, we might answer—as we do in the case of "2 + 3 = 5"—that our existence seems too obvious to require justification. Perhaps that is why Descartes writes in the *Rules* that "everyone can mentally *intuit* that he himself exists, that he thinks, that a triangle is bounded by three sides, that a sphere has a single surface, and so on" (*Rule II,* AT 10:368). At least when he wrote the *Rules* (probably in the late 1620s), he seems to think that the basis for our knowledge of our own existence is similar to that for our knowledge of simple geometric truths.

Accordingly, on one reading of *Meditation II,* which I will call the intuitive interpretation, the Cogito passage simply reports Descartes' having intuited that he exists.

While consonant with what he writes in the *Rules,* the intuitive interpretation seems to conflict with much of what he writes elsewhere. In the Cogito itself, for example, he says that he has weighed every consideration and that he is forced to conclude that the proposition "I am" is true (AT 7:25). In *The Search after Truth,* he talks about the Cogito's reasoning [*ratiocinium*] (AT 10:523). In the *Principles,* he calls "I am" a conclusion (*Princ. I,* 9, AT 8:7). In *Replies II,* he says that "I am" is deduced from "I think" (AT 7:140), and in *Replies V,* he talks about the inference from "I think" to the conclusion "I am" (AT 7:352). Unless Descartes misunderstood what he was doing, it seems clear from what he says that there is an inferential movement in the Cogito and that the Cogito therefore is not simply the report of a simple intuition.

The Cogito as Evidential Inference

Some of Descartes' contemporaries, including the authors of *Objections II,* suggest that the Cogito contains the following argument:

4.1. Whatever thinks exists.
4.2. I think.
4.3. Therefore, I exist.

Conclusion 4.3 does seem to follow validly from premises 4.1 and 4.2, and, while Descartes does not actually state premise 4.1 in the Cogito, it seems to be an obvious truth of the sort that people often take for granted.

At this point in the *Meditations,* however, Descartes is still dealing with the doubts of *Meditation I.* In particular, having explicitly called such propositions as "2 + 3 = 5" into doubt with the hypothesis of the evil demon, he refuses to assert these propositions and others that seem equally self-evident. Precisely because such propositions seem self-evident, the Demon's Advocate believes them to be false, and Descartes' rule at this point in the *Meditations* is to assert that *p* only if he can convince the Advocate that *"p"* is true (Chapter 3). But, if Descartes' method requires that he withhold assent from the proposition "2 + 3 = 5," doesn't it also require—for exactly the same reason—that he withhold assent from premise 4.1, "Whatever thinks exists"? Surely the Advocate would argue that, since it seems obviously true to him that whatever thinks exists, and since his mind is systematically misdesigned, premise 4.1 must be false.

Aware of this problem, Descartes writes in *Replies II,*

When someone says "I think; therefore I am or exist," he does not deduce existence from thought by means of a syllogism, but recognizes it as something self-evident by a simple mental intuition. This is clear from the fact that, if he were deducing it by means of a syllogism, he would have to have previous knowledge of the major premise "Everything that thinks is or exists." (AT 7:140)

Then perhaps the reasoning is just this:

4.2. I think.
4.3. Therefore, I exist.

The argument from 4.1 and 4.2 to 4.3 fits the familiar pattern in which a general rule is applied to a particular case, while the shorter argument from 4.2 to 4.3 does not. Still, the shorter argument is valid if the longer one is. If the premise "Whatever thinks exists" expresses a necessary truth, as it seems to do, the possible worlds in which the premises of the longer argument are true are exactly the same as those in which the premise of the shorter argument is true. And an argument is valid just in case every possible world in which its premises are true is also one in which its conclusion is true.

There seems to be ample evidence that, in the Cogito, Descartes does deduce 4.3 from 4.2. In the passage quoted earlier from *Replies II,* for instance, he explicitly says that he infers "I am" from "I think" and uses the formula "I think; therefore I am or exist" to record the Cogito's reasoning (AT 7:140). But how does this reasoning figure into the Cogito? A typical use of arguments is to record the relation of one's evidence for a proposition to the proposition itself. (So, for instance, if my evidence that my right hand exists is that I see it, I might say, "I see my right hand; therefore, it exists.") Accordingly, noting that Descartes constructs the argument from 4.2 to 4.3 in the Cogito, it's natural to suppose that he offers the fact that he thinks as evidence for the claim that he exists. Since people often marshal evidence for their beliefs in the attempt to become certain, it's also tempting to suppose that, in the Cogito, Descartes tries to find such strong evidence for his own existence that he becomes perfectly certain of it.

When this interpretation is brought into the light, however, its problems become obvious. If an argument's premises record our sole evidence for its conclusion, the argument warrants perfect certainty regarding its conclusion only if we are perfectly certain of the truth of its premises. In particular, if "I think" records Descartes' only reason for believing that he exists, the argument from "I think" to "I am" can establish its conclusion with perfect certainty only if, before constructing the argument, he is perfectly certain that he thinks. But, in *Meditation I,* he has gone through elaborate reasoning to show that all his beliefs are subject to doubt. If we take him to be certain of "I think" as he writes the Cogito, we should at least expect him to discuss the certainty of this proposition, carefully justifying the view that it is beyond doubt. When we look at the Cogito, however, it seems that the single "fixed and immovable" point on which he intends to build his system is "I am," not "I think." Indeed, in the Cogito itself, Descartes never even asserts that he thinks; when the phrase "I think" does appear, it is grammatically subordinated, tucked away in longer sentences primarily about his existence: "Let [a deceiver] deceive me all he can, he will never make it the case that I am nothing while I think that I am something. . . . [So,] I must finally conclude that the statement 'I am, I exist' must be true whenever I state it or mentally consider it" (AT 7:25). Perhaps a case can be made that "I think" can be known with perfect certainty prior to "I am" and that other propositions—such as "I am"—can be inferred with perfect certainty from it, but the fact is that Descartes makes no attempt to construct such a case. In *Meditation II*, "I am" is in the spotlight, while "I think" is hardly visible in the background—not at all where we would expect to find the first proposition rescued from the doubts of *Meditation I*.

The moral to be drawn, I suggest, is that, while the argument "I think; therefore, I exist" does figure into the reasoning of the Cogito, its function is not to record Descartes' evidence that he exists. After discussing another interpretation of the Cogito, I will point to another function that it might serve.

The Cogito as Performance

Having considered the intuitive interpretation of the Cogito and the inferential interpretation, I will now briefly consider Hintikka's performative interpretation.[2]

At the heart of this interpretation is the concept of an "existentially inconsistent sentence." To say that a sentence is logically inconsistent is to say that, in using it, one makes a statement that somehow conflicts with itself and which therefore cannot possibly be true. In contrast, to say that a sentence is existentially inconsistent is to say that, in using it, a person makes a statement that conflicts, not with itself, but with the truth that the person who states it exists. An obvious example of such a sentence is "I do not exist." If, say, Descartes were to use this sentence in the usual way, the statement he would make would be that Descartes does not exist—a statement that, though logically consistent, must be false whenever Descartes himself makes it. Since anyone can use the pronoun "I" to refer to him or herself, the point can be generalized: Whenever anyone asserts "I do not exist," what he or she says must be false. As Hintikka puts the point, existentially inconsistent sentences—such as "I don't exist"—defeat themselves whenever they are uttered.

At the outset of the Cogito, through the device of the Demon's Advocate, Descartes forces himself to assert the contrary of much of what he once believed. According to Hintikka, Descartes here attempts to assert the contrary of "I am," but he finds himself unable to do so. The explanation for this inability, says Hintikka, is that "I do not exist" is an existentially inconsistent sentence. Accordingly, on this interpretation, it is the existential inconsistency of "I do not exist" that places the proposition "I am" beyond the doubts of *Meditation I.*

This interpretation seems supported by the passage in the Cogito where Descartes writes, "The statement 'I am, I exist' must be true whenever I state it or mentally conceive it" (AT 7:25). Yet, like the other interpretations I have considered, it faces problems.

First, on this interpretation, Descartes does not infer "I am" from "I think" (or from anything else), and advocates of this interpretation therefore have difficulty dealing with the numerous passages in which Descartes seems explicitly to say that the Cogito does involve such an inference. Hintikka himself discounts these passages, contending that Descartes was only dimly aware of the nature of his own reasoning. The use of the term *therefore* in "I think, therefore I am" is "peculiar," says Hintikka, and the entire formula is a "misleading" summary of Descartes' insight.[3] While Descartes may not have understood his own reasoning perfectly, it seems to me that the number of places in which he definitely states that the Cogito contains an inference weigh heavily against the performative interpretation.

Second, the performative interpretation does not, by itself, explain why Descartes viewed "I am" as perfectly certain. Suppose for the sake of argument that this interpretation is right—that Descartes recognizes "I do not exist" as an existential inconsistency and that he therefore finds himself unable to assert that he does not exist. It follows that Descartes should view the proposition "I am" as undeniable. But undeniable propositions are not necessarily perfectly certain. Notice, for example, that while Descartes says that he "recognizes an obvious inconsistency" in the proposition "2 + 3 = 5," he still manages to call this proposition into doubt. He cannot prevent himself from believing that 2 + 3 = 5, and he therefore finds it undeniable that 2 + 3 = 5. Yet, as I argued in Chapter 1, the hypothesis that his mind is poorly designed provides him with grounds for doubt.

If the logical inconsistency of "2 + 3 = 5" doesn't rescue that proposition from the doubts of *Meditation I,* why should the existential inconsistency of "I do not exist" place Descartes' existence entirely beyond doubt? If his inability to deny that 2 + 3 = 5 does not entail that he is perfectly certain that 2 + 3 = 5, why should his inability to deny that he exists entail that he is perfectly certain that he exists? As far as I can see, the performative interpretation of the Cogito offers no answers to these questions.

Broughton's Suggestion

On another interpretation of the Cogito, which has been developed by Janet Broughton, Descartes rescues "I am" from the doubts of *Meditation I* by noting that "his existence [was] a condition for his having carried out the intellectual activity he described in the First Meditation." According to Broughton, the logic behind the rescue is this:

Suppose I am considering a class of beliefs about which I can have at most only one reason for doubt. Now suppose I somehow managed to show that I could have such reason for doubting a particular belief—the belief that [*p*]—only if that very belief were true. By recognizing this, I would be able to see that I cannot rationally doubt whether ["*p*"] is true: I would be able to be absolutely certain about ["*p*"].[4]

In effect, Broughton asks us to view Descartes as reasoning like this in the Cogito:

4.4. I can have grounds for doubting that I exist only if I do in fact exist.
4.5. Therefore, there are no rational grounds for my having doubts about my existence.

Having reached 4.5, says Broughton, Descartes has attained perfect certainty concerning his own existence.

While rejecting what I have called the intuitive and argumentative interpretations of the Cogito, Broughton views the passage as containing an argument—in my formulation, the argument from 4.4 to 4.5—and her reading therefore faces a question similar to that faced by other argumentative interpretations of Cogito: As Descartes begins *Meditation II,* can he affirm 4.4 without violating the rules of his own method? He has just called the Demon's Advocate into existence and resolved not to enter any proposition into his new system of beliefs unless he can convince the Advocate of its truth. But, if the Advocate were asked whether 4.4 were true, he might reason like this: "It seems obviously true to me that I can have grounds for doubt only if I exist. But my mind is so poorly designed that what seems most obviously true to me is in fact false. Therefore, 4.4 is false."[5]

Another, equally important, problem with Broughton's interpretation of the Cogito is that she doesn't explain why we should view the argument from 4.4 to 4.5 as valid. From 4.4, together with the obvious fact that he doubts, Descartes can infer that he exists and that "I am" is true. But how does that help him to evaluate the argument from 4.4 to 4.5? Neither the fact that "I am" is true nor the fact that Descartes believes it to be true entails that he can't have any doubts about his own existence. Then why think that 4.4 does entail 4.5?

To see that this is not an idle question, consider Descartes' position in the middle of *Meditation I*, after he has introduced the hypothesis of the evil demon but before he has resolved to withhold his assent from each of his beliefs as if it were false. Presumably, at this point, he would accept and assert 4.4. How could he doubt unless he existed? On the other hand, at this point in the *Meditations*, he has in mind a hypothesis (namely, the hypothesis of the evil demon) such that (i) he has some suspicion that it might be true and (ii) it seems to him that it challenges his belief that he exists.[6] At this point in the *Meditations*, the doubts created by the consideration of the hypothesis of the evil demon seem to him to be rational: since he cannot conclusively rule out that hypothesis, and since it seems to him that the hypothesis challenges each of the propositions that he views as most obviously true, it seems to him that he has "valid and well-considered grounds" for doubt [*validae et meditatae rationes*] (AT 7:21). Thus, it might seem to Descartes when he reaches the middle of *Meditation I* that the argument from 4.4 to 4.5 is invalid. At this point in the *Meditations*, we can suppose, he accepts 4.4, while he rejects 4.5 because he has grounds for doubt concerning each of the propositions that seem most obvious to him, including "I am."

Broughton might reply that the doubts that the hypothesis of the evil demon produce in Descartes concerning his own existence are not *rational,* in the sense of that term required for 4.5—that, while it may initially seem to Descartes that he has rational grounds for doubts concerning his own existence, such doubts are in fact ill-founded. Perhaps; Descartes' aim in the Cogito, after all, is to show that there is something incoherent with the thought that he can doubt his own existence. But, if *rational* is taken in this way, what would warrant Descartes' moving from 4.5—"There are no rational grounds for my having doubts about my existence"—to the conclusion that he is perfectly certain that he exists? As long as it *seems to him* that he has grounds for doubt concerning his own existence, he is not perfectly certain that he exists—even if those grounds eventually prove in some way to be irrational. Together, my analyses of being perfectly certain (Chapter 2) and of having doubts (Chapter 1) entail this, since they explain what it is for a person to have doubts in terms of what seems to that person to be the case. And this is as it should be. Could we make any sense out of someone's saying both that, although it seems to him that he has grounds for doubt concerning a proposition, he is perfectly certain of that proposition's truth?

Unlike advocates of the intuitive and argumentative interpretations of the Cogito, Broughton correctly notes that the point of the passage is not simply to establish that "I am" is true, but to show that it is indubitable—that we cannot have any grounds for doubt concerning our own existence. She also correctly notes that, rather than being viewed in isolation from the project of the *Meditation,* the reasoning of the Cogito should be seen as arising out of Descartes' method of doubt. The shortcoming of her position, I suggest, is that it does not adequately explain *how* the certainty of the Cogito does arise from the doubts created in *Meditation I.*

Dispelling Doubts with the Cogito

Having raised problems for several interpretations of the Cogito, I will now sketch a reading that avoids the problems of the intuitive, inferential, and performative interpretations without turning its back on their insights. For reasons that will emerge, I will call this reading the doubt-dispelling interpretation.

One thing that seems clear about the Cogito is that, by the end of the passage, Descartes claims perfect certainty concerning his own existence. As an approach to doubt-dispelling interpretation of the Cogito, then, I will look back to the test for perfect certainty that Descartes established in *Meditation I*.

Consider once again the fictional person whom I have called the Demon's Advocate. As I explained in Chapter 3, the Advocate is very much like Descartes. In particular, his Will is compelled to affirm the same propositions as Descartes' Will and his judgment on the validity of arguments is the same as Descartes'. The relevant difference is that, while Descartes believes his powers of intuition to be generally reliable, the Advocate believes that his mind is the product of an evil demon who is determined to deceive him. Accordingly, confronted with a proposition "*p*" that Descartes finds undeniable, the Advocate will generally argue like this:

4.6. Proposition "*p*" seems obviously true to me (as it does to Descartes).

4.7. My mind is so poorly designed that what seems obviously true to me is in fact false.

4.8. Therefore, proposition "*p*" is false.

At this point in the *Meditations*, Descartes does not have any way conclusively to rule out premise 4.7, and imagining the Demon's Advocate therefore allows him to counterbalance the inclination to affirm the propositions that seem to him most obviously true.

But let's consider the argument from 4.6 and 4.7 to 4.8 when the proposition in question is "I am":

4.6'. The proposition "I am" seems obviously true to me (as it does to Descartes).

4.7. My mind is so poorly designed that what seems obviously true to me is in fact false.

4.8'. Therefore, the proposition "I am" is false.

What Descartes notices in the Cogito, I suggest, is that even the Demon's Advocate should find this argument unacceptable.

To see why, suppose that a computer has been programmed so that, when a sentence from a given list is inputted, the computer outputs "true" if and only if the inputted sentence is false. Generally, if we know that the computer has been programmed this way, we can infer that a sentence is false if we receive the response "true" upon typing that sentence into the computer. But now suppose that we find the sentence "This computer exists" on the list, that we type it in, and that we get the response "true." Following the general pattern, we might try to infer that the sentence "The computer exists" is false and, accordingly, that the computer does not exist. While such an inference might be valid, there clearly would be something wrong with it. Fully explicated, the inference would rest on premises about the computer's programming—sentences that presuppose or entail that the computer does exist and hence that the sentence "The computer exists" is true. And such premises can validly entail that the computer does not exist only if those premises are inconsistent. But an argument with inconsistent premises is unsound, and an unsound argument does not provide us with reason for accepting its conclusion. So, despite the initial appearances, the fact that the computer returned the output "true" would not give us good reason for thinking that the sentence "The computer exists" is false.

The Demon's Advocate judges an argument to be valid just in case Descartes does, and Descartes clearly judges the argument from "I think" to "I am" to be valid. But it seems to Descartes that premise 4.7 entails that the Demon's Advocate undergoes mental processes and, hence, that he thinks, in the broad Cartesian sense of *think*. Accordingly, the Advocate will accept the inference from 4.7 to "I am" as valid. And, having done so, he will have to reject the argument from 4.6' and 4.7 to the conclusion that "I am" is false (4.8'). It would be just as unreasonable for him infer that "I am" is false from 4.6' and 4.7 as it would be for us to infer, on the basis of the computer's returning the result "true" when we typed in "The computer exists," that the computer does not exist. Since the premises of his inference would seem to him to entail that he does exist, it would be reasonable for him to take 4.8' to follow validly from those premises only if he admitted that some of those premises were false, and an argument with false premises would not provide him with any grounds on which to affirm its conclusion.

But does 4.7 entail "I am"? At least one commentator on the *Meditations* has suggested that the answer is no. Hamlet had many thoughts, writes Hintikka, but he did not exist.[7] The argument from "Hamlet thinks" to "Hamlet exists" is therefore invalid (the reasoning continues), as is the analogous reasoning from "I think" to "I am."

While the question of the logical validity of the argument from "I think" to "I am" may be intrinsically interesting, it seems to me to be irrelevant to the reasoning of the Cogito. In *Meditation I,* Descartes does not simply announce that he is going to question all of his beliefs. Rather, he accepts the burden of showing that each of those beliefs is dubious. To shoulder this burden, he introduces the hypothesis of the evil demon, which provides him with grounds for doubt concerning various propositions because (i) he has some (very slight) suspicion that it may be true and because (ii) it seems to him to challenge those beliefs. But for reasons that I have outlined, the hypothesis of the evil demon does not seem to Descartes to challenge his belief that he exists. On the contrary, it seems to him to entail that he does exist; "Surely, I exist," he writes in *Meditation II,* "if I am deceived" (AT 7:25). Accordingly, what Descartes shows in the Cogito is that even the hypothesis of the evil demon does not provide him with grounds for doubt concerning "I am."

Descartes therefore seems to have accomplished what initially appeared impossible: he has found a proposition *"p"*—"I am"—such that he is (strongly) inclined to believe that *p* and has no grounds for doubt concerning its being the case that *p*. The source of the inclination has remained the same all along; he intuits that he exists. What has changed is that, in the Cogito, he has demonstrated that the hypothesis of the evil demon, which initially seemed to provide grounds for doubt concerning each of the propositions whose truth he intuits, does not really provide any grounds for doubt concerning this proposition.

I say that Descartes seems to have accomplished this because there are logical questions here to which I do not pretend to have answers. Obviously, the language in which he asserts that $2 + 3 = 5$ stands to the language in which the Advocate asserts that the proposition "$2 + 3 = 5$" is false as object-language to metalanguage. Similarly, if "I am" is in the object-language when Descartes asserts it, proposition 4.7 (namely, "My mind is so poorly designed that what seems obviously true to me is in fact false") is in the metalanguage, as is "I am" when deduced from those premises. Accordingly, the language in which Descartes asserts "I am" is logically distinct from the language in which the Advocate asserts "I am." Then can we say that, in asserting "I am," Descartes expresses exactly the same proposition as the Advocate expresses with those words? Regardless of the answer acceptable to modern logicians, there is clearly an intuitive pull toward saying that in the Cogito, when debating the Demon's Advocate, Descartes is holding a debate with *himself* on the question of whether he exists and accordingly that, if he can convince his opponent that he (the Advocate) exists, he (Descartes) has established that he (Descartes) exists. I also suggest that, for the reasons I have outlined, once Descartes thinks that he has won this debate, he thinks that he has rescued "I am" from the doubts raised in *Meditation I*. Since Descartes and the Advocate are in agreement concerning Descartes' existence, and since the consideration of the Advocate provided Descartes with his only counterbalance to his belief that he exists, he thinks that he no longer has any grounds for doubt concerning his own existence, and hence that he has established the proposition "I exist" with perfect certainty—even though he has not discovered any new reason for thinking that he exists.

This reading of the Cogito is consistent with the tenet of the intuitive interpretation that (as Descartes writes in the *Rules*) "everyone can mentally intuit that he himself exists." On the intuitive interpretation, however, the fact that Descartes intuits his own existence suffices by itself to rescue "I am" from the doubts of *Meditation I* and to establish that proposition with perfect certainty. The problem, which I outlined above, is that there are other propositions whose truth Descartes intuits—such as "2 + 3 = 5"—which he continues to doubt until *Meditation III*. What rescues "I am" from the doubts of *Meditation I*, I suggest, is not the fact that we intuit its truth, but the fact that it bears a certain logical relation to the doubt-producing hypotheses of *Meditation I*. While these hypotheses clearly seem to Descartes to entail "I am," they do not (or at least do not seem to Descartes) to entail other intuited propositions (such as "2 + 3 = 5"), which therefore remain in doubt.

To derive "I am" from the doubt-producing hypotheses of *Meditation I*, Descartes notices that these hypotheses entail that he engages in mental activity—or, in other words, that he thinks, in the broadest sense that term. And, from the proposition that he thinks, he infers that he exists. The doubt-dispelling interpretation of the Cogito can therefore account for passages that seem to favor the inferential interpretation of the Cogito over the intuitive—passages in which Descartes argues from the premise "I think" to the conclusion "I am." But, on the inferential interpretation, Descartes constructs this argument to *prove* that he exists, and "I think" records his *evidence* for believing that he exists. On the doubt-dispelling interpretation, he constructs this argument simply to establish that the relation of entailment holds (or, more precisely, seems to him to hold) between the doubt-producing hypotheses of *Meditation I* and the proposition "I am." So, unlike the inferential interpretation, the doubt-dispelling interpretation avoids the embarrassment of needing to explain how Descartes could have established his first perfectly certain belief—namely, the belief that he exists—by inferring it from other, prior beliefs.

Finally, the doubt-dispelling interpretation agrees with the performative interpretation in that, on both, Descartes asserts "I am" in *Meditation II* because he finds it impossible reasonably to do otherwise. On the performative interpretation, this is because he is aware that "I do not exist" holds the special status of an "existentially inconsistent sentence." But why, then, does he point to the logical relation of "I think" to "I am"? And why does the "existential inconsistency" of "I am not" rescue "I am" from doubt, when the conceptual inconsistency of "The square does not have four sides" fails to rescue the proposition "The square has four sides"?

On the doubt-dispelling interpretation (as on Broughton's), what rescues "I am" from doubt is not its own logical or linguistic status, but its special relation to the hypotheses that Descartes used to raise doubts in the first place. Unlike "The square has four sides," the proposition "I am" seems to Descartes to follow immediately from the doubt-producing hypotheses of *Meditation I*. But, as I have argued, once we see that these hypotheses entail a proposition, they no longer provide us with grounds for doubt concerning that proposition's truth.

Sum Res Cogitans

Should we say that, having definitely concluded that "nothing [he] used to believe is beyond legitimate doubt" in *Meditation I*, Descartes retracts that conclusion in the Cogito? Perhaps. He did not explicitly consider his belief that he existed in *Meditation I*, and no harm would be done by his saying later that he had simply overlooked the fact that the reasoning of *Meditation I* had failed to call "I am" into doubt. But Descartes also has another, more interesting reply (which is important for the proof of dualism in *Meditation VI*). What has happened in *Meditations I* and *II* has so altered his idea of himself that the belief he would have expressed with the words "I am" before beginning the *Meditations* differs from the one he expresses with the same words after the Cogito. The first belief, he might say, was called into doubt in *Meditation I*, while the second was not even framed until *Meditation II*.

As Descartes points out, he begins *Meditation I* with a confused conception of his own nature:

> I will now look at the thoughts that spontaneously and naturally occurred to me when I reflected on what I was. The first thought to occur to me was that I have a face, hands, arms, and all the other equipment (also found in corpses) that I call a body. The next thought to occur to me was that I take nourishment, move myself around, sense, and think—that I do things that I trace back to my soul. Either I didn't stop to think about what this soul was, or I imagined it to be a rarified air, or fire, or ether permeating the denser parts of my body. (AT 7:26)

Obviously, the idea of himself that Descartes here describes is closely bound up with the idea of body.

Until *Meditation VI*, Descartes (speaking as the Demon's Advocate) denies the existence of bodies. Yet, as I have explained, the Cogito forces even the Demon's Advocate to affirm that he exists. So, at this point in the program of the *Meditations,* the Advocate's position is that, although he exists, there is no physical world. If this position is inconsistent, Descartes does not seem to see the inconsistency—at least at this point in project. (If he did, he could point it out to the Advocate, who agrees with him on all points of logic.) But to say that Advocate's position seems consistent is to say that the Advocate can—and, indeed, has—conceived of himself without conceiving of himself as a physical object. If his *only* idea of himself were the idea of a body, the proposition "I exist, but there are no bodies" would be as obviously inconsistent and untenable as the proposition "My foot exists, but there are no physical objects."

By playing the part of the Demon's Advocate, Descartes has therefore modified his idea of himself. At least in *Meditation II,* he must conceive of himself in entirely mental terms, simply as a thinking-thing [*res cogitans*]:

I am not now admitting anything unless it must be true, and I am therefore not admitting that I am anything at all other than a thinking thing—that is, a mind, soul, understanding, or reason (terms whose meaning I did not previously know). I know that I am a real, existing thing, but what kind of thing? As I have said, a thing that thinks. . . . And what is that? Something that doubts, understands, affirms, denies, wills, refuses, and also senses and has mental images. (AT 7:28)

Descartes goes on in *Meditation II* to admit that he may in fact be a body and that he may have properties that are not strictly mental. ("Might it be that [physical objects] which I do not yet know about and which I am therefore supposing to be nonexistent really aren't distinct from the 'I' that I know to exist? I don't know, and I'm not going to argue about it now" [AT 7:27].) For the moment, however, his project requires that he conceive of himself without attributing anything to himself but thinking, and—on his own account—that is what he does.

Thus, in *Meditation II,* Descartes develops a new conception of himself, which he isolates, through the fiction of the Advocate, from all ideas of body. If believing involves affirming a mental proposition and mental propositions are made up from ideas, there is therefore a point to saying that the belief Descartes would have expressed in *Meditation I* with the words "I am" is distinct from the one he would express after the Cogito with the same words. And, if these beliefs are distinct, Descartes can say that, while he has grounds for doubting the first, he holds the other with perfect certainty—at least after he has convinced the Demon's Advocate that there could not be a sound argument whose premises include proposition 4.7 ("My mind is so poorly designed that what seems obviously true to me is in fact false") and whose conclusion is that "I am" is false.

CHAPTER 5

From Self to God

At the end of *Meditation II*, "I am" is the only proposition of which Descartes is perfectly certain, and, consequently, the only proposition that he has admitted into his developing system. While there may be some intrinsic philosophical interest to knowing that perfect certainty is attainable, the project of the *Meditations* would be a dismal failure if he could go no further. Descartes' aim, after all, is not simply to demonstrate the theoretical possibility of perfect certainty, but to develop a system of perfectly certain beliefs broad enough to provide a basis for reclaiming or replacing many of the beliefs that he abandoned in *Meditation I*.

At the center of any such system, says Descartes, is the proposition "God exists." As he sees it, only by arguing that there is an omniscient, omnipotent, and benevolent God can he conclusively refute the doubt-producing hypotheses of *Meditation I* and silence the Demon's Advocate.

In this chapter, I will focus on *Meditation III*'s arguments for God's existence. Temporarily abstracting these arguments from the project of the *Meditations*, I will postpone the discussion of many important issues—including the crucial issue of how Descartes can justify asserting the premises of these arguments even though the Demon's Advocate would view them as false.

Semidistinctness

Descartes' first argument for God's existence rests on his conception of substance, which is in turn based on the thought (derived from Suarez)[1] that identity and distinctness can be defined in terms of ontological independence. (See *Princ. I*, 60, AT 8:28–29.)[2] According to this theory,

5.1. Thing *A* is identical to thing *B* just in case it's logically impossible for *A* to exist without *B* and for *B* to exist without *A*,

and

5.2. Thing *A* and thing *B* are really distinct just in case it's logically possible both for *A* to exist without *B* and for *B* to exist without *A*.

While these principles entail that a thing *A* and a thing *B* cannot simultaneously be both identical and distinct, they do not rule out the possibility that they might be neither—as would be the case, for example, if thing *B* could not possibly exist without thing *A* while *A* could exist without *B*. To designate the relation of such things to one another, I will coin the term *semidistinct*:

5.3. *B* is semidistinct from *A* just in case it's logically possible for *A* to exist without *B* although it's logically impossible for *B* to exist without *A*.

If we regard dents as things in the relevant sense of that term, for instance, a dent in a fender is semidistinct from the fender. As the fender once existed without the dent and might exist without it in the future, it's logically possible for the fender to exist without the dent. Yet the dent could not possible exist without the fender. The dent, we might say, derives its existence from that in which it is a dent.

So defined, identity, real distinctness, and semidistinctness relate to methods of counting. Often, we count *A* and *B* as one if they are identical and as two if they are numerically distinct.[3] But, if *B* is semidistinct from *A*, we don't count them either as one or as two. Although we can count dents and we can count fenders, we don't count the fender and the dent as one thing (partly because they are things of very different sorts), and we don't them as two either (partly because the dent can't exist independently of the fender).

In the *Principles* (*Princ. I*, 61, AT 8:29), Descartes discusses a species of semidistinctness that he calls "modal distinctness." In one form,[4] the modal distinction is "the distinction of a mode, properly so called, from the substance of which it is a mode." We can grasp what Descartes means by "mode" here by considering one of his examples: the square shape of a stone is a mode of that stone (*Med. III*, AT 7:45). When we say that a substance has a certain *attribute*—when, for example, we say that a body has the attribute of extension without saying anything about its particular size or shape—we do not assert that the substance is limited or bounded. In contrast, according to Descartes, when we predicate a mode of a substance, we describe a "defect or limitation of perfection" (*Replies II*, AT 7:161). According to his theory, to say of a table that it has the mode of being three feet long is to say that it falls short of infinite extension in a certain way.

On the picture of substance and quality familiar, say, from Locke's *Essay Concerning Human Understanding*,[5] the sentence "The table is three feet long" is true just in case a real quality—namely, the quality of being three feet long—is present in the table. But, according to Descartes' theory, the sentence "The table is three feet long" is true just in case an attribute—namely, full and unbounded extension—is *absent* from the table in a certain way. Since the limitations of a substance can't possibly exist without the substance itself, the modal distinction is a species of what I am calling semidistinctness.

But does Descartes view modal distinctness as the only species of semidistinctness? That is, from the fact that *B* is ontologically dependent on *A*, does it follow that *B* is a mode of *A*? At first glance, certain sections of the *Principles* (*Princ. I*, 60–62, AT 8:28–31) may suggest that he does. Here, where he seems to be striving to make an exhaustive list of forms of diversity, modal distinctness is the only item on the list that can be regarded as a species of semidistinctness. Yet there are obvious examples of semidistinctness that are not examples of modal distinctness. A hole in a sheet of paper is semidistinct from the sheet although the hole is not one of the sheet's modes. More important for purposes of understanding *Meditation III*'s arguments for God's existence, since Descartes believes that the things that he calls "created substances"—such as his own mind and the physical objects around him—could not possibly exist without God's bringing them into existence moment by moment, he seems committed to the view that such things are semidistinct from God. But created substances are things rather than modes. Indeed, Descartes says that God, a being in whom limitation is inconceivable, doesn't have any modes (*Princ. I,* 56, AT 8:26).

Three Senses of *Substance*

Using the notion of semidistinctness, we can distinguish at least three senses in which Descartes uses the term *substance.*

First, he applies the term *substance* to an entity if it is not semidistinct from anything. Thus, he writes that a substance is "a thing that so exists that it needs nothing else to exist" (*Princ. I,* 51, AT 8:24). To mark this sense of the term *substance,* I will use the phrase "primary substance." By the end of *Meditation III,* Descartes believes himself to have shown that there is exactly one primary substance, God, and that the existence of everything else depends at every moment on God's bringing it into existence at that moment.

Second, Descartes applies the term *substance* to things that are semidistinct from God but not from anything else—that is, to things that derive their existence immediately from God. Believing that human minds and bodies require nothing else to exist but "the help of God's concurrence," he calls such things "created substances"—a phrase that he frequently abbreviates simply to *substances.* (See, for example, *Med. III,* where he calls a stone a substance without using the qualifying term *created* [AT 7:44–45].)

Third, with respect to given entity or property, Descartes applies the term *substance* to anything from which that entity or property is semidistinct. Thus, in *Replies II,* he offers the following definition:

The term [*substance*] applies to everything in which something that we perceive resides immediately as in a subject, or to everything by means of which something that we perceive exists. By "something that we perceive," I mean any property, quality, or attribute of which we have a real idea. The only idea we have of a substance itself, in the strict sense, is that it is the thing in which something we perceive . . . exists, either formally or eminently. (*Definition V,* AT 7:161)

To mark this sense of substance, I will use the phrase "supportive substance."

For reasons that are unclear, Descartes seems to think that the only possible tiers of existence are those of primary substance, created substance, and properties of created substance. So, on his view, a supportive substance is either a primary substance or a created substance. And, on his view, both primary substances and created substances are supportive substances. According to the metaphysics at which he hints in the *Meditations,* the attribute of extension exists (eminently)[6] in God, and, on the definition of *substance* from *Replies II,* having an attribute (even eminently) is a sufficient condition for being a supportive substance. Created substances, such as rocks, obviously are supportive substances, since they have various properties. So *supportive substance* seems to be an overarching term that applies both to God and to creative substances. It therefore is no surprise that, within a page of defining *substance* as that in which properties, qualities, or attributes reside, Descartes writes that God is the substance that we understand to be absolutely perfect and that a body is a substance in which we find shape, motion, and so on (*Definitions VII* and *VIII,* AT 8:162). If he uses the term *substance* in one sense in one definition and another sense in the next, there is no hint of the shift in the text.

In the *Principles,* however, Descartes insists that there is no sense of *substance* in which it applies both to God and to created substances (*Princ. I,* 51, AT 8:24). Reconciling this passage with what he says in *Replies II* would be difficult, if not impossible. But, fortunately, present purposes do not require the attempt. Whether or not Descartes recognizes a sense of *substance* in which the term applies both to God and to created substances, it seems clear that, when he calls God a substance (meaning that He is a primary substance) and minds or bodies substances (meaning that they are created substance), he uses the term *substance* in two different senses.

Fixing on this fact, commentators on Descartes' metaphysics are inclined to infer that the two uses of the term are unrelated. Anthony Kenny writes, for example, that "created substances are not logically, but causally, dependent on God, [since] they do not inhere in God as a subject, but are effects of God as a creator."[7] It's true, of course, that Descartes thinks that God stands to everything else as a creator stands to his creation and that he views God's relation to created things as *causal* in some sense of that term. But according to Descartes, God is the *causa in esse* of created things, not their *causa in fieri* (*Replies V,* AT 7:371)—that is, He is something whose existence at a given moment makes the existence of other things possible at that moment, not something that produces things in the way, say, that a human craftsman produces artifacts. (It is, I will argue, partly to insist on this point that Descartes offers a second argument for God's existence in *Meditation III*.) So, by itself, that God's relation to the created world is causal does not entail that it is contingent rather than necessary, any more than the fact that the stone is the *causa in esse* of its squareness entails that the squareness is contingently rather than logically dependent on the stone.

Also, Descartes contends that God's essence is absolute perfection (*Med. III,* AT 7:65; *Replies II,* AT 7:162)—that God's nature is to be infinite, independent, supremely intelligent, and supremely powerful primary substance (*Med. III,* AT 7:45). When he notices about himself that he is imperfect (for example, in *Med. III,* AT 7:45–46), he therefore is not merely noticing that, as a matter of contingent fact, he is not God—in the way, say, that I might notice that, as a matter of contingent fact, I am not the president of the United States. Rather, he is noticing that his essence (whatever it might be) differs from the essence of primary substance and hence that he is of the wrong ontological type—or as he might say, the wrong degree of reality—to be God. Being a created substance, he is something that cannot possibly exist on his own.

As R. S. Woolhouse notes, "there is no evidence that [Descartes] confusedly thought that the dependence of created substances on God was of the same kind as that of modes on substances."[8] Indeed, by explicitly denying that God has modes (*Princ. I,* 56, AT 8:26), Descartes seems to go out of his way to insist that the two forms of dependence differ. But it's one thing to deny that these forms are the same, and another to deny that they are similar. And there are several reasons for thinking that Descartes did think that, in some ways, God's relation to created substances resembles the relation of created substances to their modes.

First, as I have argued, Descartes viewed both the relation of God to created substances and the relation of created substances to their modes as forms of what I have called semidistinctness. From this basic similarity, we might suppose, others follow.

Second, as I have mentioned, Descartes recognized three "degrees of reality": God, created substances, and properties of created substances.

If the relation of God to created substances differed fundamentally from the relation of a created substance to its modes, there would be no single axis running through this hierarchy.

Third, there is the obvious fact that Descartes applies the word *substance*—often without a modifier such as *created*—both to God and to created substances. (In *Meditation III,* for example, he boldly says, "I am a substance" [AT 7:45].) This double use of the term *substance* invites us to think of God and created things as similar. In particular, since Descartes thinks of substance as that which grounds the existence of other things (as when he uses *substance* to mean "supportive substance"), his use of the term *substance* invites us to view God as standing to His ontological dependents (at least in some respects) as created substances stand to their properties or modes. It would have been a mistake for Descartes to issue this invitation if he didn't intend us to accept it—a mistake of the sort that he seldom makes.

Fourth, and most important, we can make better sense of *Meditation III*'s primary argument for God's existence if we view Descartes as assuming that God stands to created substances (roughly) as created substances stand to their modes. At first sight, his argument seems to rest on counterintuitive premises—such as "Our conception of the infinite is prior to our conception of the finite" and "Everything present in an effect must be present in its cause"—that he offers without much explanation or support. But as I will argue, we can construct plausible arguments for these premises if we view him as projecting some of what he believes about the familiar relation of created substances to their modes onto the relation of God to His creations.

Unlike Spinoza,[9] Descartes thinks that the analogy breaks down; being perfect and eternal, God cannot have any modes, since modification implies limitation and mutability. But to say that an analogy breaks down is not necessarily to deny that it is useful.

God as Substance

The conception of God suggested most naturally by the Old Testament is that of a person who walked in the Garden of Eden, talked to Adam and Eve, negotiated with Lot, and spoke to Job out of the whirlwind. The conception suggested by the New Testament is that of a compassionate and benevolent father. At least on the surface, Descartes' conception of God is less personal and more abstractly metaphysical—the so-called God of the Philosophers. "By 'God,'" Descartes says in *Meditation III*, "I mean a *substance* that is infinite, independent, supremely intelligent, and supremely powerful—the thing from which I and everything else that may exist derive our existence" (AT 7:45). And, in *Replies II*, in a list of formal definitions, he writes, "The *substance* that we understand to be supremely perfect and in which we conceive absolutely nothing involving defect or limitation of its perfection is called God" (AT 7:162).

Why did Descartes think that he could reduce the question of whether there is a God to the question of whether there is a primary substance?

An obvious part of the answer lies in the place Descartes gives to primary substance in his ontology. The Judeo-Christian conception of God is that of a being who existed prior to everything else, the Creator of the heavens and earth. If there were exactly one primary substance, it would be ontologically prior to everything else, and everything else would derive its existence from it.

Another, less obvious part of the answer has to do with how Descartes links his idea of God to his idea of himself. His contention is not just that he has an idea of a primary substance, but that he has the idea of a primary substance from which his mind—the thinking thing whose existence he established in *Meditation II*—is semidistinct. For reasons that I will outline later, he holds that everything present in him would have to be present to an infinite extent in a primary substance from which he derived his existence. But, in proving his own existence, he has established that he knows some things, that he has the ability to act, and that he possesses some goodness. So, as he sees it, the conception of a primary substance from which he derives his existence must be the conception of something with infinite knowledge, power, and goodness—something resembling the Judeo-Christian God.

The Ultimate Standard of Comparison

The starting point of Descartes' primary argument for God's existence is the premise that he has an idea of God. If we conceive of God as a heavenly father, it seems uncontroversial that we do have a conception or mental image of Him. But, as Descartes uses the term *idea*, to say that a person has an idea of an object *x* is to say that an entity of a certain sort comes before that person's Understanding, thereby presenting[10] *x* and enabling the person to mentally grasp *x*. By insisting that God is infinite, however, Descartes seems to suggest that a finite human mind cannot contain an idea of Him. Then why does he think that he does have an idea of God?

Descartes offers an answer to this question in *Meditation III:* "It's clear to me that . . . my grasp of the infinite must somehow be prior to my grasp of the finite—my understanding of God prior to my understanding of myself. For how could I understand that I doubt and desire, that I am deficient and imperfect, unless I had the idea of something more perfect to use as a standard of comparison?" (AT 7:45–46). The thought here seems to be that the idea of the finite presupposes the idea of the infinite—that we could not have ideas, say, of our own limited selves unless we first had an idea of God, a being infinite in the various respects in which we as created substances are finite.

This thought has historical precedent. (When Boethius argued for God's existence, for instance, he appealed to the principle that we can conceive of an imperfect thing of a kind only if we conceive of a perfect thing of that kind.)[11] Still, the view that the idea of the infinite is prior to the idea of the finite seems paradoxical. What seems likely, at least to modern thinkers, is that we arrive at the idea of the infinite by extrapolation on the idea of the finite, not that we arrive at the idea of the finite by limitation of the idea of the infinite.[12]

Descartes' theory of substance leads him in another direction. Since the idea of his self that he developed in *Meditation II* is the idea of a being that doubts and wants, and since the idea of primary substance must be the idea of something perfect and infinite, he can conclude that his idea of himself is not the idea of a primary substance—the only other possibility being that it is the idea of something semidistinct from primary substance. But, as he insists in his argument for dualism (*Med. VI,* AT 7:76), if we can (clearly and distinctly) conceive of *B*'s existing without *A*, it's logically possible for *B* to exist without *A*. And this entails that, if it's logically impossible for *B* to exist without *A*—for example, if *B* is semidistinct from *A* in the way in which Descartes conceives of himself being semidistinct from God—we can't conceive of *B* without conceiving of *A*. Reasoning of this sort led Descartes to the conclusion that we cannot conceive of a mode of a created substance without conceiving of the created substance itself. (See, for instance, *Princ. I*, 61, AT 8:29, and *Princ. I*, 64, AT 8:31.) And analogous reasoning may have led him to the conclusion that we cannot conceive of ourselves without conceiving of a primary substance from which we are semidistinct.

But, even if we grant that we can't conceive of ourselves as finite beings without conceiving of a primary substance, why should we admit that we can't conceive of ourselves as finite beings without conceiving of a primary substance that is *infinite* or *boundless?* Perhaps the answer rests, again, on the analogy to created substances. In *Meditation II,* when Descartes considers a piece of wax in isolation from everything semidistinct from it, he finds that it does not per se have any bounds to its extension; boundaries imply modes, which he has conceptually set aside (AT 7:31). Similarly, viewed in itself, primary substance would be without bounds. So, while the idea of a primary substance may be the idea of something with attributes (such as mentality and agency), these attributes must be conceived as present in it without limitation.

In fact, this is not quite the route that Descartes takes in *Meditation III* to the conclusion that we cannot conceive of created substances without conceiving of infinite primary substance—perhaps because he tries in the *Meditations* to avoid the details of his theory of substance. Instead, in *Meditation III,* his argument rests on the premise that he could not "understand that [he is] deficient and imperfect" unless he had "the idea of something more perfect to use as a standard of comparison" (AT 7:45–46).

Imagine a music teacher who is attempting to develop in a student the concept of playing in tune. Apparently, it won't do for the teacher to demonstrate playing out of tune in several ways and then to add that playing in tune is not like that—for, however many ways the teacher plays out of tune, there will be others. But it might do for the teacher to play in tune and to tell the student that anything else is out of tune. In some way, the idea of playing in tune is primary and the idea of playing out of tune secondary. We might say that the idea of playing in tune provides a standard by comparison to which scales are judged out of tune. Descartes' view, as I understand it, is that his idea of perfect, infinite substance stands to his idea of himself as the idea of an in-tune scale stands to the idea of an out-of-tune scale.

Descartes might try to support this view by pointing to the theory of predication that I attributed to him earlier. On this theory, to say that object *A* has a property *P* is (at least in cases where *P* is a mode) just to say that *A* falls short of infinity or perfection in a certain way. For example, according to this theory, to say that a table is three feet long is just to say that the table falls short of infinite extension in a particular way, *W.* It's a small step from this theory of predication to the doctrine that to think that the table is three feet long is simply to think that the table falls short of infinite extension in way *W*—mentally to compare the table to an infinitely extended thing and to note the differences. But it seems that we cannot mentally compare one thing to another unless we have ideas of both. So Descartes' theory of predication suggests that, in order to think that the table is three feet long, one must have the idea of something that somehow contains unbounded extension.

Generalizing from this reasoning, Descartes might infer on the basis of his theory of predication that one cannot have the idea of any finite thing (*qua* finite) unless one has the idea of an infinite thing of the same sort. An instance of this general principle is, of course, that he could not "understand that [he] doubt[s] and desire[s], that [he is] a deficient and imperfect unless [he] had the idea of something more perfect to use as a standard of comparison" (AT 7:45–46). Perhaps that is why he held the (notorious) view that the idea of God is innate. On the theory of mental predication that I have attributed to him, the idea of the infinite is always epistemologically prior to the idea of the finite and imperfect. So, on this theory, if we are not born with the idea of the infinite in us, we must at least acquire it as a prerequisite to having any other ideas.

True, in the project of the *Meditations,* Descartes examines his idea of himself before he moves on to the idea of God. But this may be because he wants to use the contention that he has a clear and distinct idea of himself as a premise of his argument to the conclusion that he has an idea of God—not because he thinks that he has an idea of himself prior to having idea of God. To those who insist that God is ineffable and hence that we have no genuine idea of Him, Descartes responds, in effect, that he developed an idea of myself in *Meditation II* and that he could not have done so unless he already had an idea of God.

Degrees of Reality

From the premise that he has an idea of God, Descartes attempts to move to the conclusion that God does in fact exist. Yet he himself demonstrates at length that, generally, arguments of the form "I have an idea of *x;* therefore *x* exists" are invalid. "As to my ideas of other people, animals, and angels," he writes, "it's easy to see that—even if there were no people but me, no animals, and no angels—I could have composed these ideas from those that I have of myself, of physical objects, and of God" (AT 7:43). And he goes on explicitly to apply the same thought to his ideas of size, shape, motion, color, sound, odor, shape, taste, heat, substance, duration, and number.

To justify the inference from "I have an idea of God" to "God exists," Descartes therefore points to something unusual, if not unique, about his idea of God: its "degree of reality." Many commentators have recoiled at this notion. "Everything that exists has full reality," they say, "and nothing else has any reality at all (since there is nothing else)." Thus, in *Objections III,* Hobbes writes, "Does reality admit of more and less? . . . If [Descartes] thinks that one thing can have more reality than another, he should consider how this can be explained to us with the clarity that every demonstration demands and that he himself achieves elsewhere" (AT 7:185). But, granted the notion of semidistinctness, Descartes *can* explain what he means by saying that one thing has a higher degree of reality than another: the degrees of reality are simply steps on the ladder of ontological dependence. Despite Hobbes's protests, it seems natural to say, as Descartes does in *Replies II,* that "substance has more reality than accident or mode" (AT 7:165)—that a stone has more "thinghood" [*realitas*] or "entity-hood" [*entitas*] than the shape of that stone. If we find that something stands to the stone as the stone stands to its shape, it would be natural to view that thing as having a higher degree of reality than the stone. (And, if we find that something stands to the stone's shape as the shape stands to the stone, it would be natural to view it as having a lower degree of reality than the shape.)

That commentators often have a hard time seeing this may, in part, be a problem of translation. There is no better English translation for *realitas* than "reality," and, when we say in English that something has reality, we may mean nothing more than that it exists. But the Latin *real* is the adjectival form of the *res*, which means "thing." To say that *A* has *realitas* is therefore to say that, to some degree, it is thinglike—which, according to Descartes, is to say that, to some degree, it is ontologically independent of other entities.

For Descartes' argument in *Meditation III,* the crucial question is whether there is something on which his self and other such entities are ontologically dependent—something above the level of his self from which that self is semidistinct. To show that there is and complete his argument for God's existence, he must move from the premise that he has the idea of such a thing to the conclusion that it exists.

Kinds of Reality

Since Descartes views his ideas as modes of his mind, he admits that they are at a lower level of reality than his mind. But he also contends that, since the object of one of his ideas is something at the ultimate degree of reality, that object must be at the ultimate degree of reality, even if it only exists as an object of his thought. To defend this view, he appeals to a doctrine of three kinds of reality or presence: formal, eminent, and "objective" (or, as I will sometimes say, reality as object of thought).[13] Occasionally he writes as if these distinctions applied to entities or substances, but, for understanding his argument for God's existence, it's useful to think of it as applying to properties, essences, or (as Descartes sometimes says) natures.

The least controversial way of being is the formal. To say that a nature has formal reality is to say that it is manifest in the temporal order, and, in the case of physical objects, in the spatiotemporal order. A property has formal reality just in case it resides in a formally existing entity in such a way as to warrant our straightforwardly attributing that property to that entity. To say that the table formally possesses the property of squareness, for instance, is to say that the table exists and that the property of squareness is related to it so as to warrant our saying that the table is square.

According to Descartes, something is said to exist *eminently* in the objects of our ideas when, "although not present in the way that we perceive it, it is there with sufficient strength to take the place" of what would be present in that way (*Replies II,* AT 7:161; *Princ. I,* 17, AT 8:11). That is, according to Descartes, an attribute sometimes exists in a substance in a way that does not entitle us to attribute that property to the substance but that still explains how the substance can bestow that property on its effects. (Since Descartes eventually concludes that God creates the physical world, and since he subscribes to the view that everything present in an effect must be present in its cause, he needs the notion of eminent reality to avoid the conclusion that God is an extended and hence divisible entity.) That he offers very little explanation of eminent reality is unimportant for present purposes, since the concept of eminent reality does not figure importantly into the arguments of the *Meditations.* Indeed, in all of *Meditation III,* where the doctrine of kinds of reality has center stage, the term *eminent* appears only four times, none of them important for the "proofs" of God's existence.[14]

The burden of Descartes' argument in *Meditation III* falls on the manner of presence that he ranks lowest—what I have called "existence as an object of thought." If to say that *A* exists as an object of thought were merely to say that we think of *A,* Descartes' talk about existence of this sort would be uncontroversial. But from "*A* exists as an object of thought," he wants to draw inferences that do not obviously follow from "I am thinking of *A*" alone. In his view, when a nature exists as an object of thought, it has a mental presence, and it therefore requires a cause of the same sort that would be needed to manifest that nature formally. "However imperfect the existence of something that exists objectively in the understanding through an idea," he writes in *Meditation III,* "it obviously is something, and it therefore cannot come from nothing" (AT 7:41).

Caterus, the author of *Objections I,* disagrees. "Why," he asks, "should I seek the cause of something that is not actual—something that is just a name, is nothing?" (AT 7:92). Descartes' answer rests, I suggest, on a philosophical picture of ideas that is crucial to his primary argument for God's existence.

In his reply to Caterus, Descartes distinguishes the sun in the sky from the idea of the sun on obvious grounds. The sun in the sky is a physical object "located outside our understanding," but the idea of the sun is something that "can never exist outside an understanding" (*Replies I*, AT 7:102). Either of these entities could exist without the other. (If we were thinking about the sun when it disappeared from the sky, the sun still might remain the object of one of our ideas, and, if we were to go out of existence, the sun might cease to be an object of our ideas even though it continued to exist in the sky.) In addition, the sun in the sky is a created substance, while Descartes' idea of the sun seems to be a mode of the created substance that is his mind. Descartes therefore seems committed to the view that the idea of the sun and the sun in the sky are really distinct from one another.

Yet in a passage that some dismiss as a slip of Descartes' pen, he draws a different conclusion: "The idea of the sun *is* therefore the sun itself existing in the understanding, not formally as it does in the sky, but objectively—*i.e.*, as things generally are in the understanding. This way of being is much less perfect than that in which things exist outside the mind, but it is not on that account absolutely nothing, as I have already said" (*Replies I*, AT 7:102–3). In what sense of *is* can Descartes plausibly say that the idea of the sun is the sun itself? According to a doctrine of natures (which Descartes sketches in the *Rules* and mentions in *Replies I*), there is something—namely, the nature of the sun—that can manifest itself in the world in several different ways. This nature manifests itself in the spatiotemporal order as the brightest object in the daytime sky and, at the same time, it manifests itself in the world as an object of thought. While the two manifestations are distinct in that either could exist without the other, *what* is manifest is the same in both cases. Since the sun in the sky is the nature of the sun manifesting itself in the physical world while the idea of the sun is the same nature manifesting itself as object of thought, a relation akin to identity must hold between them.[15]

In some ways, this relation resembles that of a particular performance of Beethoven's Fifth Symphony to a printed copy of the symphony's score. Although the performance and the score are not entities of the same type, they present one and the same piece of music. Focusing on what is presented rather than the manner of its presentation, we might point to either and say, "That is Beethoven's (one and only) Fifth Symphony." Similarly, if I see a building in the morning and a photo of it in the afternoon, I might point toward the photo and say, "That is the same building I saw this morning"; the photo presents the building to me, though not of course in the same way as concrete and glass.

However philosophically problematic this view may be, it has an intuitive attraction, especially once we have resolved to analyze thought in terms of ideas. It seems natural to suppose that, when the idea of the sun comes before our minds, our thoughts are *of* a certain physical object, which I have called the sun in the sky. But what is it about this idea that makes it an idea of that object? Besides facing Berkeley's objection that nothing but an idea can possibly resemble another idea,[16] the assertion that the idea resembles its object fails to explain how one of my ideas might be of the sun even if it pictures it inaccurately (say, as a small, shiny disk) and therefore resembles something else (say, the small, shiny disk on my desk) much more closely than it resembles the sun. Descartes' view, as I understand it, sidesteps all such difficulties (while perhaps opening other metaphysical cans of worms). According to Descartes, an idea so presents its object that, in the way I have described, the presentation can be said to *be* that object.

Of course, on this theory, the two manifestations of the nature of the sun differ in their media: one is mental and the other physical. And there is another difference, more important to Descartes' argument for God's existence. When the nature of the sun manifests itself as a physical object, it does so in such a way as to warrant the attribution of that nature, and of the properties that comprise it, to the object. For instance, when the nature of the sun manifests itself in the physical world, the entity in which it manifests can correctly be said to be hot. In contrast, when the nature of the sun manifests itself in a mind as an idea, the idea cannot be said to be hot. In Descartes' language, the nature manifests itself formally in one case and "objectively" in the other.[17]

Descartes therefore believes that there are two independent axes on which we can assess an idea's reality, one having to do with degrees of reality and the other having to do with kinds of reality. According to

Descartes, if one of our ideas is of a certain entity, that entity is present as an object of the idea, and such presence is less perfect than formal or eminent being. On the other hand, the object of an idea has its own degree of reality, which has to do with the object's nature rather than with the manner of its manifestation. While placement on the first axis has to do with *how* the nature is manifested, placement on the second axis is determined by *what* is manifested.

In effect, in the following passage from *Meditation III*, Descartes places his idea of God on these two axes:

Insofar as the ideas of things are just modifications of thought, I find no inequality among them; all seem to arise from me in the same way. But, insofar as different ideas present different things to me, there obviously are great differences among them. The ideas of substances are unquestionably greater—or have more objective reality [that is, reality as object of an idea]—than those of modifications or accidents. Similarly, the idea by which I understand the supreme God— eternal, infinite, omniscient, omnipotent, and creator of all things other than Himself—has more objective reality in it than the ideas of finite substances. (AT 7:40)

Descartes here contends that, in his idea of God (which is a mode of his mind), the ultimate degree of reality (that is, the reality of primary substance) appears as an object of his thought—which is to say that, in this idea, the most perfect nature appears in the least perfect way.

Regardless of how this nature appears, the fact is that it does appear. "My idea of God," he might have said in *Replies I*, "is God himself, appearing in the way that things generally present themselves to my understanding." Therefore, despite the manner of God's presence in my ideas, that presence requires a cause. From examining its effect, what can we tell about this cause?

Causal Principles

To move from his belief that God is present in one of his ideas as an object of thought to the conclusion that God exists formally, Descartes appeals to the principle that everything in an effect is present in its cause—a principle that he regards as a corollary to the venerable dictum "Nothing comes from nothing" (AT 7:40). But why grant that this principle is true? While flipping a switch may not be in itself catastrophic or beautiful or long lasting, it can have catastrophic, beautiful, or long-lasting effects if the switch is wired to the right equipment. Then why couldn't God as object of idea have something imperfect as its cause?

Descartes answers with a homey analogy: "How could a cause give something," he writes in *Meditation III*, "unless it itself had it?" (AT 7:40). But this answer seems to beg the question by assuming that everything present in an effect must have been given to it by its cause. When flipping the switch causes a catastrophe, there doesn't seem to be any reason for saying that the properties of the catastrophe were given to it by the switch flipping.

The problem here arises from a misunderstanding. When Descartes writes about the cause of his idea of God, he is not thinking of an object or event existing before the idea that somehow forced the idea into existence. Rather, as I have argued, when he talks about the relation of cause to effect in *Meditation III,* what he has in mind is the relation of a thing *A* to something semidistinct from *A*. As I've said, an example of such a relation is that of a created substance to a mode of that substance—the relation, say, of a stone to that stone's mode of squareness. But Descartes thinks that to say of a substance that it has a certain mode is to describe a way in which that substance is limited—a way in which it falls short of perfection. Consequently, according to Descartes, nothing can be present in a mode that was not present in the substance of which it is a mode. If *B* arises from *A* by diminution, how could anything positive be present in *B* that was not present in *A*?

My suggestion is that, while Descartes denies that God has modes, he views the semidistinct relation of a mode to a created substance as so similar to the semidistinct relation of his self to God that he is willing to argue by analogy from one to the other. In particular, noting that the mode of squareness in the stone arises by limitation of the (determinable) extension in the stone, he reasons that his self is a diminished and limited image of God, the primary substance from which his self is semidistinct.

A thing might, of course, have properties that are not present in a substance from which that thing is semidistinct. (For instance, a dent in a fender might be square while the fender itself is not.) But, as I have explained, on Descartes' theory of predication, much of what we say about objects has to do with ways in which they *fall short* of perfection—with absence or privation [*privatio*] rather than with positive presence. Accordingly, despite his doubt, dependence, limitation, powerlessness, and moral imperfection, Descartes is not committed to the conclusion that God, the cause of his existence, is imperfect. All he denies is that, if *A* is semidistinct from *B*, there can be something *positive*, such as mentality or spatial extension, that is present in *A* but not in *B*.

God's Formal Reality

For the moment, let's grant Descartes that his idea of God has a cause that somehow contains infinite perfection and reality. To reach the conclusion that God exists (formally rather than just as an object of an idea) he must show that the cause for whose existence he has argued has the nature of God in it in a way that warrants our attributing that nature to it—that is, that the cause of his idea of God has God's nature in it formally.

Sometimes Descartes suggests that this step is so obviously valid that it requires no justification. In *Meditation III*, for example, he states, with no explicit justification, that "as an idea contains one particular mental reality rather than another, it must get this reality from a cause having at least as much *formal* reality as the idea has reality as object of thought" (AT 7:41).

Although the reality that I'm considering in my ideas is just reality as an object of thought, I ought not to suspect that it can fail to be in an idea's cause formally—that it's enough for it to be there as an object of thought. For, just as the objective existence of my ideas belongs to the ideas in virtue of their natures, the formal existence of the ideas' causes belongs to those causes—or, at least, to the first and foremost of them—in virtue of the causes' natures. (AT 7:42)

But either something that exists as an object of thought has existence of some sort, or not. If it does, why *can't* it be a cause—at least of an effect that exists only as an object of thought? On the other hand, if something that exists merely as an object of thought does not have existence of any sort, why suppose—as we must for Descartes' argument—that such a thing requires a cause?

Perhaps because he has no ready answers to these questions, Descartes grants in *Meditation III*—for the sake of argument—that something that exists merely as an object of thought might be the cause of something else of the same sort. Still, he argues, if we begin with such an object and trace the chain of causes back from it, we will eventually find a cause possessing formally everything that the effect contained objectively: "Although one idea may arise from another, this can't go back to infinity; we must eventually arrive at a primary idea whose cause is an 'archetype' containing formally all the reality that the idea contains as an object of thought" (AT 7:42). The reasoning here seems to rest on the premise that, when we trace the chain of causes back from something that exists merely as an object of thought, the chain will either regress to infinity or transcend the "objective" realm and move to the formal. Believing that it "can't go back to infinity," Descartes insists that a cause must formally contain everything that appears (even objectively) in its effects.

But why should we accept this argument's initial premise? By the end of *Meditation III,* Descartes himself believes that, if we begin with something whose being is formal and trace the chain of its causes, we eventually reach an end point: God, a formally existing being who, as perfect substance, does not require any cause other than Himself. In this case, the chain of causes neither regresses to infinity nor transcends to a higher level. Then why not suppose that, if we begin from the idea of God and trace its causes, we will eventually come to something that exists only as the object of an idea but whose existence does not require a cause?

Perhaps Descartes would answer like this: Suppose that, when we begin from the idea of God and trace its causes back, we find that the chain neither regresses to infinity nor transcends to the realm of formal reality. Then either the idea of God would be something that requires no cause, or another idea would be its cause. But, if the idea of God requires no cause, it must be something that exists on its own—which is to say that, being primary substance, it would possess God's nature formally, not just objectively. On the other hand, if we suppose that the idea of God is caused by another idea, this other idea would need to possess infinite perfection and reality (since everything present in an effect must also be present in its cause). And any idea containing these properties would be the idea of God, not another idea. So (Descartes might conclude) if we trace the chain of causes back from our idea of God, we must find either that it regresses to infinity (something he rejects out of hand) or that it leads us to something possessing formally everything that is in the idea "objectively."

With some such reasoning as this, Descartes takes the final step in his first argument for God's existence, moving from the claim that the cause of his idea of God contains infinite perfection and reality objectively to the conclusion that the cause of this idea contains them formally—and hence is God Himself.

The Independence of Moments

Having completed his first argument for God's existence, Descartes goes on to construct a second. Why? If he regards the first argument as conclusive, what might a second add? In *Meditation III*, he suggests that the explanation has to do with memory:

When I attend [without care] and the images of sensible things blind my mind's eye, it's not easy for me to remember why the idea of an entity more perfect than I am must come from an entity that really is more perfect. That's why I'll go on to ask whether I, who have the idea of a perfect entity, could exist if no such entity existed. (AT 7:48)

But he does not say why he thinks that the second argument is any more memorable than the first. It may be that he simply has the second argument in mind, realizes that it rests on intuitions different from the first, and decides to present it to his readers. I suggest, however, that he uses the second argument to explain his position on the relation of the created world to God, and in particular to emphasize the semidistinctness of created substances, including his self, from their Creator.

The starting point of the second argument is a premise about time: according to Descartes, the temporal span of his life "can be divided into innumerable parts, each of which is completely independent of the others" (*Med. III*, AT 7:49). Should we take the word *innumerable* literally here, or is Descartes using hyperbole? Did he conceive of these parts as brief temporal spans or as durationless time points? If as points, did he believe the sequence of points to be dense (so that between any two points there is a third), or did he think of the points as temporal "atoms" (so that, having fixed on one point, we can meaningfully talk about the next)? On these questions, there is scholarly disagreement. But as Jorge Secada has claimed,[18] the argument of *Meditation III* doesn't rest on any particular views about the magnitude of the moments or about the density of time. The argument's premise is that *we* can divide time into non-overlapping segments—moments such that no two of them ever exist together—and that we can do so seems undeniable.

Descartes' contention is that, since these moments do not overlap, they must be independent. As an aid to understanding what this means, let $t1$ be one moment and $t2$ a subsequent moment. At least in part, what Descartes means by saying that $t1$ and $t2$ are independent is that a complete description of the world at $t1$ (that is, a complete inventory of the created substances, modes, and relations that exist at $t1$) would be logically consistent with *any* description of the world at $t2$. (Of course, if $t1$ is in 1641 and $t2$ is in 1741, the fact that the *Meditations* were originally published at $t1$ logically entails that the first edition did not come out at $t2$, but presumably the fact that a first edition of a work was brought out at time $t1$ does not count as fact exclusively about the arrangement of objects, properties, and relations *at that moment*.)

Since to explain is to make clear, a state of affairs is susceptible to explanation only if it is somehow obscure, problematic, or puzzling. What is already clear cannot be made clear. But, ordinarily, given that something exists at a moment, we do not take its continued existence (over a short time) to be puzzling. The general presumption is that, unless the situation is unusual, if something exists at a given moment, it will continue to exist for a while. By insisting that moments of time are independent, however, Descartes seeks to cancel this presumption—to establish the empty universe as the norm from which deviation is to be explained. In taking this view, he affiliates himself with Aquinas and others who are willing to ask, "Why is there now something rather than nothing?" and unwilling to accept either "There was something a moment ago" or "Why not?" as a satisfactory response.

The argument can be cast in modern terms like this: We can think of an enduring physical object as a four-dimensional entity (three dimensions being spatial and the fourth temporal), and we can then regard objects as having temporal parts, or "slices," just as we can regard them as having spatial parts. Having taken this view, we can apparently regard the table as enduring object as a construction made up from various temporal slices: the table at $t1$, the table at $t2$, and so on. But a plausible principle of causality is that a first entity cannot directly affect a second unless the first comes into temporal contact with the second—that is, unless there is a moment at which both exist.[19] But there is no time at which both the table at $t1$ and the table at $t2$ both exist. Indeed, there is no time at which the table at $t1$ and *any* temporal object slice from a moment other than $t1$ both exist. So the table at $t1$ cannot be the direct cause of the table at $t2$—or of anything else at $t2$. And the same can be said for every other temporal object slice that existed at $t1$. So nothing that exists at $t1$ can directly affect anything after $t1$. And this entails that nothing at $t1$ can indirectly affect anything at $t2$ either—for, to do so, it would have to have a direct effect on something that existed subsequent to $t1$.[20]

It might be objected that, while there is no time at which the table at $t1$ and the table at $t2$ both exist, there is another entity that does exist at both at $t1$ and $t2$—namely, the table as enduring object. The obvious reply to this objection (which I am not here endorsing) is that the table as enduring object is a something of a fiction—that temporal table slices are ontologically basic and that enduring tables are merely constructions out of them. To accept this view of enduring objects is to cancel the presumption of continued existence. And, once we have done that, the fact that an entity existed at moment t stands in exactly as much need of explanation when the object existed through an interval leading up to t as when t is the very first moment of its existence. As Descartes puts the point,

> The fact that I existed a little while ago does not entail that I exist now, unless a cause "re-creates" me—or, in other words, preserves me—at this moment. For, when we attend to the nature of time, it's obvious that exactly the same power and action are required to preserve a thing at each moment through which it endures as would be required to create it anew if it had never existed. (*Med. III,* AT 7:49)

Then, in the case of Descartes' continued existence, what is the agent of re-creation? Once we grant that Descartes is not self-creating, the argument has roughly the same structure as Aquinas' First Way.[21] Call the thing that creates Descartes at this moment G. Either G is self-creating or not. If it is, it must be primary substance and hence must be God. On the other hand, if G is not self-creating, there must be something, G', that creates G at this moment. So we can go through the reasoning again: either G' is self-creating, in which case it is God, or there is something, G'', that creates G' at this moment. At some stage in this regression, Descartes reasons, we must eventually come to God.

Why can't the regress be infinite? As Descartes notes, he is the product of his parents, they were the products of their parents, and so on. While the view that the sequence stretches infinitely back into time may be inconsistent with the biblical account of creation, Descartes does not regard it as internally inconsistent. Then why couldn't the world consist of an infinite chain of objects such that each is semidependent on something above it?

Descartes' answer has to do, I suggest, with beginnings in time. In supposing the temporal sequence of productive causes to be infinite, we view it as having no beginning. In contrast, since Descartes thinks that each moment of time is independent of all others, he believes that the world at moment t does have a temporal beginning; there were moments before t, and then t occurred. Unlike the chain of efficient causes, the ontological structure at a moment therefore seems to arise out of nothing. Believing that nothing comes from nothing, he therefore infers that, if anything at all exists at moment t, there must be something at t that is the ground of its own existence—a primary substance. And, since he believes that a cause must have in it everything that is present in its effects (even objectively), he infers that this primary substance has everything in it that he finds in himself and in his idea of God.

Finding God Within

Having "proven" the existence of a self-creating entity, Descartes argues that he is not such an entity and hence that he is not God:

If I derived my existence from myself, I wouldn't doubt, or want, or lack anything. I would have given myself every perfection of which I have an idea, and thus I myself would be God. I shouldn't think that it might be harder to give myself what I lack than what I already have. On the contrary, it would obviously be much harder for me, a thinking thing or substance, to emerge from nothing than for me to give myself knowledge of the many things of which I am ignorant, which is just an attribute of substance. Surely, if I had given myself that which is harder to get, I wouldn't have denied myself complete knowledge, which would have been easier to get. Indeed, I wouldn't have denied myself any of the perfections that I grasp in the idea of God. None of these perfections seems harder to get than existence but, if I had given myself everything that I now have, these perfections would have seemed harder to get than existence if they were harder to get—for in creating myself I would have discovered the limits of my power. (AT 7:48)

It would be harder to create one's self than to give one's self perfections such as omnipotence and omniscience, Descartes says, and whatever can succeed at a harder task can also succeed at an easier one.

At first glance, this maxim may seem obviously, perhaps even trivially, true. Isn't it obvious that a person who can perform the difficult task of lifting a hundred pounds can perform the easier task of lifting fifty pounds? Still, there are people who can solve difficult mathematical problems although they cannot perform such easy tasks as poaching eggs, and there are people who can do the seemingly impossible—walk on fire, sleep on beds of nails—even though they cannot perform the easier task of riding a bicycle.

Of course, if we were able to sit back, design ourselves, and create ourselves according to our design, we would do our best. But the hypothesis that we are self-creating does not entail that we have designed ourselves. It simply amounts to the hypothesis that we exist on our own, without being dependent on anything at a higher degree of reality. So there is a gap in the reasoning. To bridge it, Descartes needs to justify the inference from "I am not perfect" to "I am not self-creating."

Again, Descartes' justification rests on his theory of substance: if, at any moment, he brings himself into existence, he must be a primary substance—and, as I argued, his theory of substance entails that a primary substance is infinite and perfect. Perhaps he does not explicitly offer this argument in the *Meditations* because he has adopted a conversational tone. Or perhaps at this point his project he does not want to try to establish a controversial metaphysics of substance. In any case, noting that he is imperfect, he infers that he is not self-creating and consequently that something outside him must re-create him at every moment at which he exists.

Yet, as I have argued, Descartes views himself as semidistinct, rather than really distinct, from God. And if *B* is semidistinct from *A*, *B* is neither numerically identical to *A* nor numerically distinct from *A*. Descartes' conception of God as primary substance therefore seems to commit him to the view that he is neither one and the same being as God nor another, second entity. Asked whether he is God, Descartes should, it seems, refuse to answer either yes or no. While this may seem paradoxical, it accords with orthodox theological positions. On the one hand, if Descartes were to say that he is God, he would commit the sin of hubris, claiming to be divine. On the other hand, if he were to say that he and God are two distinct entities, he might also be accused of hubris for claiming to be on an ontological par with God—another being who (though much greater and more powerful than he is) is just another person.

Descartes' belief that he is semidistinct from God has a consequence regarding the source of his knowledge of God, which he draws out in the following passage from the end of *Meditation III*:

> It's not at all surprising that in creating me God put [the idea of Himself] into me, impressing it on His work like a craftsman's mark, which needn't be distinct from the work itself. The very fact that it was God who created me confirms that I have somehow been made in His image or likeness and that I grasp this likeness, which contains the idea of God, in the same way that I grasp myself. Thus, when I turn my mind's eye on myself, I understand, not just that I am an incomplete and dependent thing that constantly strives for bigger and better things, but also that He on whom I depend has all these things in Himself as infinite reality rather than just as vague potentiality and that He therefore must be God. (AT 7:51)

Descartes points here to the biblical passages in which it is repeatedly said that God made man in His image (Genesis 1:26–27). Believing that this image "contains the idea of God," he concludes that he can arrive at an idea of God by "turning his mind's eye onto [him]self" and that he therefore grasps the idea of God "in the same way that [he] grasp[s] himself."

Augustine reports in the *Confessions* that, when he looked for God outside himself, he was looking in the wrong place. On his view, we find God by going within, as we go into our memories to find what we have forgotten.[22] But how is it possible, Augustine wonders, that we find the infinite within the finite? If the interpretation of the *Meditations* that I have offered is correct, Descartes has an answer. A created substance is not numerically distinct from the primary substance from which it is semidistinct, and we can't conceive of a created substance without conceiving of that primary substance (any more than we can conceive of a hole without thinking of the thing in which it is a hole). But the idea of primary substance obviously is not all there is to Descartes' idea of himself, which also contains the ideas of various modes and limitations. So, while primary substance may be infinite while a created substance is finite, the idea of primary substance is one component of the idea of anything semidistinct from that substance—the idea of God, one part of Descartes' idea of himself. And according to Descartes, the idea of God is God Himself, manifesting Himself in the realm of thought. So according to Descartes' theory, there is a point to saying that each thing that is able to conceive of itself has God within, where it can find Him by introspection.

There is, then, a straight line connecting Descartes' discussion of his idea of himself in *Meditation II* to the arguments for God's existence in *Meditation III*. According to Descartes, he could not have developed the idea that he has of himself unless he had the idea of God, and he could not have had that idea unless God—an infinite, primary substance from which he (and every other created substance) derives its existence—existed formally.

CHAPTER 6

The Validation of Intuition

Near the beginning of *Meditation III*, Descartes notes that he "spontaneously bursts forth" with the affirmation of obvious truths like "2 + 3 = 5" whenever he thinks of them (AT 7:36). And, as he insists in *Replies II,* if *"p"* is a proposition of this sort, he cannot doubt that *p* (AT 7:145). Still, as I explained in Chapters 1 and 2, to become perfectly certain of such propositions, he must rule out the hypothesis of the evil demon, depriving himself of even the slightest suspicion that it might be true. To this end, he attempts in *Meditation IV* to show that the hypothesis is incompatible with the conclusion, reached in *Meditation III,* that God exists.

After examining this reasoning, I will consider an objection to it that was raised by Descartes' contemporaries: the objection that the reasoning is circular. To show that Descartes can defend himself against this objection, I will outline his general strategy in *Meditations III* and *IV* and relate that strategy to the fiction of the Demon's Advocate, which I introduced in Chapter 2. Finally, I will address the thought that Descartes' reply to the objection of circularity commits him to unacceptable "psychologism."

God and the Evil Demon

Although Descartes' refutation of the hypothesis of the evil demon is crucial to the project of the *Meditations,* its statement spans just a few sentences:

Wherever there is fraud and deception, there is imperfection, and, while the ability to deceive may seem a sign of cunning or power, the desire to deceive reveals malice or weakness and hence is inconsistent with God's nature. Next, I find in myself the ability to judge that, like everything else in me, I've gotten from God. Since He doesn't want to deceive me, He certainly hasn't given me an ability that will lead me wrong when properly used. (AT 7:53–54)

According to the arguments of *Meditation III,* God is omniscient, omnipotent, and perfectly moral. He doesn't deceive unknowingly, he doesn't need to deceive, and he doesn't want to deceive. But, according to Descartes, God Himself has designed the process through which our Understandings sometimes compel our Wills to affirm propositions. If that process ever caused us to affirm false propositions, Descartes says, God would be a deceiver.

Immediately after constructing this argument, Descartes goes on to write, "There could be no doubt about this—except that it seems to imply that I don't err at all. For, if I've gotten everything in me from God and he hasn't given me the ability to err, it doesn't seem possible for me ever to err" (AT 7:54). Descartes' announcement here is that he sees only one objection to his position—namely, that it seems to run counter to the obvious fact that we do sometimes err. Much of *Meditation IV* contains his reply to this objection, which is in essence that responsibility for our errors is our own, not God's. In creating the world, God created beings who are imperfect, such as humans.[1] Having infinite Wills but limited Understandings, we sometimes choose to affirm propositions that our Wills are not compelled to affirm, and this is the source of error. Since our affirmation of these propositions arises from our own free choice rather than from an irresistible God-given disposition, God is not in any way to blame if it happens that the affirmations are false. God is not deceiving us; we are, in a way, deceiving ourselves.

While Descartes seems to think that this reply answers the only plausible objection to the argument at the beginning of *Meditation IV,* there is another, to which he might not have a ready reply. As I argued in Chapter 5, he takes himself to have shown in *Meditation III* that his mind derives its existence from God in roughly (though not exactly) the way in which a mode derives its existence from a created substance. But, even if we grant this, does it follow that the mechanism of our minds is God-given, in the sense of that term that his argument requires?

Some traditional explanations of how an imperfect world could have derived from a perfect God center on the thought that, while God himself could not have created something bad, he could have created things less perfect than He is, which could go on to create bad things.[2] Descartes himself calls such a thought to mind when, in *Meditation I,* he imagines that he is the product of an evil demon (who may himself be a creation of God), and he reminds us of this thought again when, in the second half of *Meditation IV,* he suggests that God created morally imperfect humans, gave us free will, and then watched us misuse that freedom—for example, to affirm false propositions that we do not fully understand. But, if Descartes subscribes to this picture of God's relation to his creations, how can he rule out the possibility that God created an evil demon, endowed that demon with free will, and then watched as *it* produced a poorly designed instrument for the detection of truth—namely, the human mind? If God bears no responsibility for the mistakes that *we* commit through the misuse of our freedom of choice, why would He bear responsibility for the errors that a *demon* might make when constructing our minds?

Perhaps Descartes would try to answer this question by pointing to differences between human error and errors of the sort a demon might make in constructing our minds. In the *Meditations,* the human errors under consideration generally involve the affirmation of false propositions. And, when people affirm false propositions, they themselves pay the penalty of having false beliefs. The arrangement seems fair in that wrongdoers suffer the consequences of their own wrongdoing. In contrast, if human minds were the product of an evil demon, the arrangement would be unfair. We innocent humans would suffer the consequences of the demon's actions. So, believing that God is perfectly just, Descartes might have reasoned that, although He might allow us to misuse our freedom of choice, He would not allow an evil demon to deceive us.

But not all our errors are purely intellectual. As Descartes notes, the Will chooses "to do or not to do," "to seek or avoid"—not just to affirm or deny (AT 7:57). Suppose, then, that a person, *A,* fires a gun, thereby intentionally and viciously killing another person, *B,* who has done nothing to deserve it. On Descartes' theory, person *A,* person *B,* the gun, and the bullet are all dependent on God, each ultimately deriving its existence from Him moment by moment. Also, on Descartes' theory, God recreates the world at every moment at which the bullet is in the air, placing the bullet on the path that leads from *A* to *B.* Yet, for all that, Descartes would deny that God, whom he views as morally perfect, is blameworthy or that the murder indicates any fault in His nature. Since person *A* acted from his own free will (Descartes would say), person *A* bears full responsibility.

Why not apply the same thought to a hypothesized evil demon? Why not suppose that, although both Descartes and demon derive their existence from God moment by moment, the demon can perform the immoral act of deceiving Descartes without God's being blameworthy? The injustice of Descartes' paying the penalty for the Demon's acts is no greater than that of *B* 's dying as a result of *A* 's actions—but Descartes presumably would not argue that, since God is infinitely just, vicious murder is impossible.

It is one thing to say that our minds are God-given in that they derive their existence moment by moment from God, who is primary substance. It is another to say that our minds are God-given in a way that places responsibility on God for the actions that arise irresistibly from the design of those minds. If the human mind were the product of an angel or demon with free will, why would God be any more responsible for its defects than for the defects in what *we* produce?

Dispelling Doubts

There is another, more obvious objection to the reasoning by which Descartes attempts to show that his mind is a reliable instrument for detecting truth. To get this reasoning started, Descartes must establish that God exists, and in his attempt to establish this, he seems, without thought or comment, to turn his back on the rules he has set for his own project. In particular, in constructing these arguments, he seems to have violated his own resolution to "withhold [his] assent from [his] former beliefs as carefully as from obvious falsehoods" (*Med. I,* AT 7:22). As he moves through these arguments, he draws freely on various premises, such as "The cause has at least as much reality as the effect." If he admits (as it seems he must) that these premises are subject to doubt when he first presents them, doesn't he also have to admit that there is room for doubt concerning the conclusion that he derives from them—namely, that God exists? And, if he has some suspicion that the proposition "God exists" is false, how can he use that proposition conclusively to rule out the doubt-producing hypotheses of *Meditation I?* Indeed, if he has any doubts at all concerning the truth of the proposition "God exists," don't the rules of his method preclude his asserting it or using it in his reasoning?

By the end of *Meditation IV,* Descartes has answers to these questions: "Having shown that God exists and does not deceive," he seems to reason, "I have conclusively refuted the hypothesis of the evil demon, which provided me with my only grounds for doubt concerning my non-empirical beliefs." But this answer seems to come too late. Apparently, he needs to justify the assertion of these premises as he uses them—not later, after using them to show that a veracious God exists.

Descartes' reasoning therefore seems unacceptably circular. Having moved from various premises to the conclusion that God exists, he seems to use the conclusion that God exists retrospectively to dispel doubt concerning the truth of those premises and hence to justify his having asserted them. It is, it seems, as if an interrogator, in doubt about a witness's testimony, took some of that witness's statements, constructed an argument from those statements to the conclusion that everything the witness said was true, and then used that conclusion to justify the acceptance of the argument's premises.

I believe that Descartes' reply to this accusation of circularity rests on his theory of the workings of the human mind.

As I said in Chapter 1, Descartes conceived of the mind as having two parts: the Understanding, which grasps propositions, and the Will, which affirms or denies them. On this theory, while these parts generally operate independently, some states of our Understandings suffice to compel affirmation by the Will. In particular, some propositions are such that, whenever our Understandings grasp them, our Wills are compelled to affirm them. For convenience, I will call such propositions *simple assent compellers.*[3]

While it's plausible that the axioms of Euclidean geometry are simple assent compellers, most of the theorems of geometry do not seem to be of this sort. For example, beginners in geometry seem able to understand the proposition "The internal angles of a triangle equal two right angles" without believing that it is true. Yet, noting that proofs are sometimes convincing, Descartes posits propositions that our Understandings compel our Wills to affirm when, and only when, those propositions come before our Understandings accompanied by an argument of a certain sort (AT 7:146). I will call these propositions *demonstrative assent compellers.*

On Descartes' theory, for any person at any given moment, there is a class of propositions that the person's Understanding compels his or her Will to affirm. This class may only contain simple assent compellers or, if the person has constructed compelling arguments, it may also contain demonstrative assent compellers.

There are various tactics that a person, *A,* might adopt if—for some reason—he or she wanted to increase the number of propositions in this class. *A* might direct attention to new fields in the attempt to develop new ideas and discover new simple assent compellers. Or, having noted that various propositions are demonstrative assent compellers, *A* might deliberately call several of these propositions to mind at once along with the compelling arguments for them. Finally, *A* might attempt to find or devise compelling arguments for propositions that did not initially compel his or her assent, thereby making those propositions into demonstrative assent compellers.

Imagine that person *A* uses these tactics to increase the number of propositions that his or her Will is compelled to affirm. *A* begins by bringing to mind several simple assent compellers and continues by attempting to construct compelling arguments from those propositions to others. Eventually, *A* may construct a system of propositions whose structure (if not content) is analogous to that of a formal geometry. The simple assent compellers with which *A* began will correspond to a geometry's axioms and postulates, the derived propositions to a geometry's theorems, and the compelling arguments to geometric proofs.

What about propositions that are obviously inconsistent with the axioms and theorems of such a geometrically structured system, such as "The square has five sides"? While Descartes does not directly address this question, I have made what seems to me the most plausible guess (Chapter 1). Since he believes that our Wills are compelled to assent to propositions like "The square has exactly four sides" whenever they come before our Understandings, he probably believes that our Wills are compelled to deny propositions like "The square has five sides," which seem plainly inconsistent with such propositions. Assent compellers are, he tells us in *Meditation III,* propositions "in whose denial [he] sees an obvious inconsistency" (AT 7:36).

In denying an empirical proposition, such as that the paper before me is blue, I might say, "I know what the world would need to be like for the paper to be blue, but I don't believe that the world is that way." Denying the negations of assent compellers seems importantly different. As I have argued, there is a point to saying that I do not fully understand, say, the proposition that the square has more than four sides: I cannot imagine or suppose or feign that that square has more or less than four sides. Accordingly, as odd as it may initially seem, in developing a "geometric" system of assent compellers, people make it the case that what once seemed to them to make perfectly good sense now seems to them to be nonsense.

Obviously, as Descartes develops his system of assent compellers, he believes each of the system's axioms and theorems. Nevertheless, he has doubts about the truth of each of these propositions (with the exception of "I am"). The model that he follows here is, after all, that of formal geometry, and in *Meditation I,* he explicitly claims that the propositions of "disciplines like arithmetic and geometry" *are* subject to doubt. Indeed, in *Meditation III,* he seems to go out of his way to remind us that, while he cannot prevent himself from believing that 2 + 3 = 5, he is not perfectly certain that "2 + 3 = 5" is true:

When I turn to the things that I believe myself to grasp very clearly, I'm so convinced by them that I spontaneously burst forth saying, "Whoever may deceive me, he will never bring it about that . . . two plus three is either more or less than five, or that something else in which I recognize an obvious inconsistency is true." Since I have no reason for thinking that God is a deceiver . . . the grounds for doubt that rest on the supposition that God deceives are very weak and "metaphysical." Still, to rid myself of these grounds, I ought to ask as soon as possible whether there is a God and, if so, whether He can be a deceiver. For it seems that, until I know these two things, I can never be completely certain of anything else. (AT 7:36)

Apparently, if the propositions of arithmetic and geometry are themselves subject to doubt, the theorems of any constructed system of assent-compelling propositions would also be subject to doubt, even if the system fit the geometric model.

Something extraordinary happens, however, when the proposition "God exists" becomes a theorem of Descartes' geometrically structured system. As he uses the term *God*, it means "the omniscient, omnipotent, perfectly benevolent being who is the creator of everything else that exists" (AT 7:39). Accordingly, from the theorem that God exists, Descartes deduces that we ourselves are created by a perfect entity and therefore that our minds are reliable instruments for the detection of truth. Since these corollaries are themselves theorems, Descartes can claim that the proposition "My mind is a reliable instrument for detecting truth" has become a demonstrative assent compeller for him. As I have argued, however, when one's Will is compelled to affirm a proposition, one can no longer feign the truth of what is obviously inconsistent with that proposition. Accordingly, when the proposition "I am the product of an omniscient, omnipotent, perfectly benevolent entity" becomes a theorem of Descartes' system, he can no longer even suspect he is the product of an evil demon or an incompetent designer or blind evolution. In the way that I have explained, the proposition "My mind is poorly designed"— which seems to him inconsistent with a proposition that he is compelled to affirm—no longer even makes sense to him.

Descartes reaches this point by deducing theorems from axioms, and he is therefore able to summarize his reasoning in a geometrical manner at the end of *Replies II*. But the system that he develops differs importantly from, say, Euclid's geometry. The underlying difference is of course that, while Euclid's system is freestanding, Descartes' is developed in the context of the metaphysical doubts of *Meditation I*. While Euclid offers his proofs to establish the truth of his theorems (or, at any rate, their derivability from his axioms), Descartes offers his arguments for the purpose of compelling his assent to their conclusions, thereby making himself unable even to understand propositions obviously incompatible with those conclusions.

We naturally think of intellectual progress as increasing the range of what makes sense to us. The student of mathematics to whom differential equations are inscrutable comes to understand those equations through a process of education, for example. But the movement in the *Meditations,* I suggest, is in the opposite direction. Initially, Descartes had some suspicion that the hypothesis of the evil demon might be true, but, by the beginning of *Meditation IV,* it no longer makes sense to him. Since his Understanding now compels his Will to affirm the proposition that his mind is the product of a perfect God, hypotheses obviously inconsistent with that proposition now seem to him to be incoherent—and advocates of those hypotheses seem no more worthy of consideration than advocates of the view that squares have five sides.

Accordingly, if the hypothesis of the evil demon provides us with our only grounds for doubt concerning assent compellers (as Descartes seems to suggest in *Meditation I*), the proposition "God exists" is such that, once our Understandings compel our Wills to affirm it, we are psychologically unable to have any doubts concerning any of the propositions that our Understandings compel our Wills to affirm. Regarding these propositions, we have attained perfect certainty.

While Descartes does not pause to reflect on this point in *Meditations III* and *IV,* he does discuss it in *Replies II*. There, challenged to respond to those who say that God may sometimes deceive humans, he replies,

What is it to us [who have understood the arguments of *Meditation III*] that someone feigns that that of whose truth we are completely persuaded appears false to God or an angel and hence is, absolutely speaking, false? What attention do we pay to that absolute falsity, when we do not in any way believe that it exists or have even the slightest suspicion that it exists? We have attained a conviction so strong that nothing can remove it, and that conviction clearly is the same as perfect certainty. (AT 7:145)

After *Meditation IV,* he finds himself unable to have "the slightest suspicion" that what his Understanding compels his Will to affirm is false, and he is therefore unable to bear the burden of calling assent compellers into doubt: "Thus, you see that, once we know that God exists, we need to feign [*fingamus*] that He deceives if we want to call what we clearly and distinctly perceive into doubt—and, since it is not possible for us to feign that he is a deceiver, we must take all such things to be true and certain" (AT 7:144). Although Descartes believes that the proposition "God exists" entails the proposition "Everything that my understanding compels my Will to believe is true," he is not making that logic point here. Rather, he is saying that, since he is psychologically unable to feign that his mind is poorly designed, he no longer has any doubts about assent compellers.

Citing the same passages from *Replies II* as I have, Harry Frankfurt argues that "Descartes' most basic and insistent occupation is with certainty itself" and that Descartes "tends to be rather indifferent to the question of whether the certain corresponds or fails to correspond with reality."[4] The position is similar to mine, and they are often confused. But there is a difference that emerges clearly if we imagine someone's straightforwardly asking Descartes (after *Meditation IV*) whether what seems true to him also seems true to God. Believing that Descartes lacks interest in this question, Frankfurt might imagine his responding, "I don't care since my concern is with certainty, not truth as correspondence with reality." Indeed, this is what Frankfurt hears Descartes saying in the passage beginning "What is it to us . . . ?" On my view, on the other hand, Descartes would answer like this: "Having focused all of my attention on the question of whether what seems true to me is absolutely true (in *Meditations III* and *IV*), I can now say with perfect certainty that what seems true to me *does* seem true to God. In fact, I now judge all contrary views to be incoherent."

That Descartes would reply this way is indicated by another passage from *Replies II:* "There is no difficulty for us if someone feigns that [what we apprehend as most obviously true] appears false to God or to an angel, because the evidence of our [mental] perception does not allow us *to pay any attention* to such a fiction" (AT 7:146). Here Descartes simply dismisses the hypothesis that what his Understanding compels his

Will to affirm is false—a fact that may seem to support Frankfurt's reading. But the reason Descartes gives for this dismissal is not, as Frankfurt suggests, that he lacks interest in truth as correspondence to reality, but that—having gone through the argument of *Meditations III* and *IV*—it no longer seems to him that there is a coherent hypothesis here to be considered.

If people who have understood and accepted the arguments of *Meditation III* and *IV* worry because others still believe there to be grounds for doubt concerning assent compellers, Descartes will reply (as he does in *Replies II*), "What is that to us, who cannot even have the slightest suspicion that they are right?" If people object that *they* can understand the hypothesis of the evil demon even if Descartes cannot, he will suggest (like a geometry teacher whose students have doubt about Euclid's theorems) that they go back and make another attempt to understand their proofs.

Accordingly, Descartes believes that he has ruled out every hypothesis that might call an assent compeller into doubt. But, as he sees it, the theses about God that he offers in *Meditations III* and *IV* are propositions that our Understandings compel our Wills to affirm. In consequence, on his theory, knowledge of God (who creates Himself) elevates *itself* to the level of perfect certainty.

Silencing the Demon's Advocate

As I explained in Chapter 3, the device of the Demon's Advocate requires that we imagine a person who closely resembles Descartes. The primary difference between them is that, while Descartes believes his mind to be the product of a benevolent God, the Advocate believes his mind to be the product of "an evil demon, supremely powerful and cunning, who works as hard as he can to deceive [him]." Reasoning from this belief, the Advocate takes a proposition's seeming true to him to show that the proposition is, in fact, false. "My Understanding compels my Will is to affirm that 2 + 3 = 5," he says, "and I therefore cannot prevent myself from believing that 2 + 3 = 5. Still, since my mind is the product of an evil demon, propositions which my Understanding compels my Will to affirm—such as '2 + 3 = 5'—must all be false."

As I have argued, Descartes' fundamental rule in *Meditations I* and *II* is "I will use a proposition in my calculations only if I can get the Demon's Advocate to admit that it is true." And, until *Meditation III*, the only proposition to pass this test was "I am." But let's suppose that the arguments of *Meditation III* do in fact compel Descartes' Will to affirm that God exists and hence to affirm that his mind is the product of a perfect being. Since a proposition is a demonstrative assent compeller for Descartes if and only if it is a demonstrative assent compeller for the Advocate, the Advocate will also be compelled to affirm that his mind is the product of a perfect being.

The surprise comes when the Demon's Advocate tries to move, as he has in the case of every other assent-compelling proposition, from the premise that his Will is compelled to affirm the proposition "God exists" to the conclusion that this proposition is false. "When I bear the arguments of *Meditation III* in mind," the Demon's Advocate might begin, "my Will is compelled to affirm that God does exist. Still, my mind is the product of . . ." Before *Meditation III*, he would finish this sentence by talking about an evil demon. After *Meditation III*, since his Understanding compels his Will to affirm that his mind is the product of a veracious God, he no longer can sincerely assert (or even pretend, suppose, or feign) that his mind is the product of such a demon. In effect, the Demon's Advocate has been silenced—at least for the moment.[5]

In Descartes' time, meditations (of roughly the same form as his *Meditations*) were used to record religious conversion. In his own way, Descartes uses the literary form for the same purpose. In his view, perfect certainty is not approached in stages; we do not become progressively more certain until we can go no further. Rather, perfect certainty comes at a single moment—the moment at which our Understandings compel our Wills to affirm that God exists. Of course, on his theory, what compels our Wills to affirm that God exists is our consideration of an argument. Reason, he would say, is the tool of conversion.

But why doesn't the Demon's Advocate object to the premises of Descartes' argument, such as "The cause must have at least as much reality as the effect"? Presumably, these premises seem obviously true to the Advocate. Otherwise, why would he eventually find Descartes' arguments for God's existence compelling? And, up to this point, the Advocate has reasoned (except in the Cogito) that, since he is the product of an evil demon, the propositions that seem obviously true to him are in fact false. Then why doesn't he reject such premises as "The cause must have at least as much reality as the effect" as they are presented, interrupting Descartes' reasoning and preventing him from completing his arguments for God's existence?

In answering, it is important to remember that the Demon's Advocate can do his job only if he remains reasonable (Chapter 3). That Descartes can imagine an irrational person who holds beliefs opposite to his own does not provide him with grounds for doubt concerning his initial beliefs or help him to withhold assent from those beliefs. What does help him counterbalance his beliefs is imagining a person who holds beliefs opposite to his own although that person is as rational and reasonable as he is. Having imagined such a person, Descartes can ask himself, "How can I claim to be certain that what I believe is true when someone as reasonable as I am (and as aware of the evidence) thinks that what I believe is false?"

But a requirement of being reasonable is that one listen to arguments with an open mind, giving others the chance to persuade. Extreme dogmatists are unreasonable, even if their beliefs are consistent—indeed, even if their beliefs are true. So the Demon's Advocate, being a reasonable person, allows Descartes to complete the arguments of *Meditation III*. By the time that he might reasonably object (Descartes thinks), he can no longer sincerely do so, since he can no longer sincerely assert the hypothesis of the evil demon.

The Charge of Psychologism

In the last section, I outlined what seemed to be several problems with the strategy of the *Meditations*. One concerned the principles about substance, reality, causation, and time that Descartes introduces in *Meditation III*. When he uses these principles as premises of arguments for God's existence, he cannot plausibly claim perfect certainty concerning their truth. Yet, because he has constructed these arguments, he claims perfect certainty concerning the proposition "God exists" and hence concerning all other assent compellers. How can an argument with uncertain premises establish that argument's conclusion with perfect certainty? The answer I have suggested rests on the thought that Descartes' aim in constructing the arguments of *Meditation III* is not to marshal evidence for God's existence, but to subtract grounds for doubt. To be useful in this subtractive process, the arguments need not have premises of which he is perfectly certain. All that is required is that they render him psychologically incapable of entertaining the hypothesis of the evil demon, thereby denying him his only ground for doubt concerning his nonempirical beliefs.

But, in taking this line against the objection of circularity, wouldn't Descartes open himself to another objection of equal gravity? As he begins *Meditation III,* he seems engaged in an uncompromising search for truth. If I have described his strategy correctly, however, the function of the arguments of *Meditation III* is to prevent him from understanding the hypothesis of the evil demon and so to rid him of doubts. Accordingly, if I have interpreted Descartes' strategy correctly, its aim does not seem to be to ensure that all his beliefs are true, but merely that he holds those beliefs with psychological certainty. Thus Kenny writes, "The veracity of God . . . is brought in [by Descartes], *not* in order to prove the truth of what I intuit, but in order to show that I shall never have reason to change my mind about what I have once intuited."[6] And Frankfurt agrees: "What [Descartes] wishes to avoid is not error, in the sense of noncorrespondence [of beliefs to reality], but betrayal. If a belief can be expected to remain unshaken by any further inquiry, that is all the truth [that Descartes] cares to demand."[7] A similar objection surfaces when another commentator gives the paragraph from *Replies II* that I quoted earlier—"What is it to is that someone feigns . . . ?"—the name "the limited aim passage."[8] The thought seems to be that Descartes faced the choice of pursuing truth or becoming certain and that, at least in this passage, he opted for the lesser good.

But, in deciding to seek certainty, *is* Descartes limiting his aims? Imagine that someone who suspects that Omaha is the capital of Nebraska goes to the library to research the matter. Suppose that, when first asked to describe his aim, this person says, "I want to find out whether it's true that Omaha is the capital of Nebraska," but that, when asked the same question a few minutes later, he says, "I want to become certain that Omaha is the capital of Nebraska." Given that to become certain that *p* is to become certain that it's true that *p,* should we say that, in the interval between the questions, this person's aims have changed? And, even if we do say this, should we view the person as having *lowered* his sights? It seems to me that, if there has been a movement, it has been in the other direction.

Still, in view of my analysis of the Cartesian aim of perfect certainty, there does seem to be a point to saying that Descartes has chosen certainty over truth. On that analysis, a person has perfectly certainty concerning the belief that *p* just in case he has conclusively ruled out every hypothesis that might provide him with grounds for doubt concerning its being the case that *p*. And, to conclusively rule out a hypothesis, I have suggested, is to work one's self into a psychological state from which that hypothesis no longer seems to make any sense. But, before completing the arguments of *Meditation III* and *IV,* Descartes does not seem to have any reason for denying that people can work themselves into such a state with regard to propositions that do make sense and are, in fact, true. It therefore seems that he does not have any reason for thinking that all the propositions concerning which he achieves perfect certainty will be true. It may be that, *after* he has completed *Meditation III,* he can argue that the existence of a veracious God ensures that all propositions of which he is perfectly certain are true—but, in *Meditation II,* he resolves to seek perfect certainty in the absence of assurances that by doing so he will avoid falsehood.

An analogy may sharpen the objection: Suppose that a mad brain surgeon has developed an operation that makes people unable to prevent themselves from believing that God exists: a doubtectomy. It might be a comfort to undergo the operation—especially if we find the doubts of *Meditation I* disturbing. Still, if nothing we know about the operation provides us with any justification for thinking that God exists, we might reasonably refuse to undergo it. The psychological certainty that the operation produced would not be warranted, and the operation itself would, it seems, be nothing more than psychological trickery. But isn't what Descartes does in the *Meditations* similar trickery, a verbal counterpart to the surgical doubtectomy?

I think not, since there are important ways in which the doubtectomy operation fails as an analogy for what Descartes tries to do in the *Meditations.*

To see one difference between the cases, notice that we would not take someone's refusal to undergo a doubtectomy to indicate a fault or vice. (If anyone would be blameworthy, it seems, it would be those who allowed themselves to undergo the operation as a way of avoiding the intellectual work involved in coming to a reasoned conclusion about God's existence.) But, in Descartes' case, the analog of refusing surgery is refusing to listen to argument—denying others the chance to persuade us through reasoning. As I explained in the last section, someone who does this *can* properly be accused of an intellectual vice: dogmatism.

A second (connected) difference between the doubtectomy and the procedure that Descartes adopts in the *Meditations* has to do with the possibility of resisting conversion. Part of what is wrong with the doubtectomy operation is that the means for producing belief circumvents the patients' critical abilities. When they awaken from anesthesia, they simply find themselves unable to withhold assent from the proposition "God exists." In contrast, in the case of the program of the *Meditations,* there is opportunity for criticism. As Descartes constructs the arguments of *Meditations III* and *IV,* he himself raises (and then answers) various objections to the reasoning. While he supposes that these arguments will eventually compel our assent to their conclusions, he does not suppose that the compulsion is so sudden and complete that it precludes criticism or rational evaluation.

And this points to a third and more general difference between the cases: The doubtectomy produces belief in an unusual, troubling way that we might with some justice call merely psychological. But according to Descartes, the way in which the arguments of the *Meditations* persuade us that God exists—though psychological in that it rests on a connection between Understanding and the Will—is no different from the way in which, say, mathematical proofs convince us of the truth of their conclusions. Since Descartes constructs the arguments of the *Meditations* to persuade, and since persuasion is a psychological process, it can hardly be an objection to his procedure that it is, in some way, psychological.[9]

Those who accuse Descartes of psychologism persist, however. "We can distinguish the pragmatic evaluation of an argument (which centers on the question of whether the argument does in fact convince)," they say, "from its logical evaluation (which centers on the question of whether it *should* convince—that is, on whether its premises are true and its reasoning valid)." "In accusing Descartes of psychologism," they continue, "we are saying that he focuses on the pragmatic evaluation of *Meditation III*'s arguments for God's existence to the exclusion of their logical evaluation."

But, in *Meditation III*, Descartes' sole aim is the construction of arguments for God's existence, not the evaluation of those arguments. When he does turn to questions of evaluation in later *Meditations,* his point is that (to some extent) questions of logical evaluation can be *reduced* to questions of pragmatic evaluation. On his view, arguments that we find irresistibly compelling must have true conclusions, since otherwise God could not be defended against the accusation that He is a deceiver. Rather than focusing on pragmatic evaluation to the exclusion of logical evaluation as the objectors contend, Descartes tries in the middle *Meditations* to connect evaluations of the two sorts—to show that the pragmatic fact that an argument compels our Will to assent to its conclusion entails the logical fact that its conclusion is true.

How we assess Descartes' attempt to establish this connection depends on whether the arguments of *Meditation III* and *IV* have succeeded in compelling our assent. If we do not find those arguments compelling, we may suspect that some of the arguments that succeed in producing complete conviction in people should not do so. On the other hand, if we do find these arguments compelling, the objection that Descartes engages in "psychologism" will seem misguided. That is, the question of whether we should aim for truth or for perfect certainty will seem important to us only if we suppose that some propositions of which we are perfectly certain might be false—a supposition that we will reject out of hand if we find the arguments of *Meditations III* and *IV* completely convincing.

As I said earlier, while Descartes' tone in the *Meditations* is more often coldly logical than emotional or devotional, *Meditation III* reports a religious conversion. The effects of this conversion are more profound than his simply changing his mind about which propositions are true and which false. Sentences that seemed to him to express intelligible propositions—such as "My mind is poorly designed"—now seem to him not to make any sense at all. There is no reason to suppose that, when he looks back over the chasm of this conversion, he will be able straightforwardly to convince those on the other side that his new beliefs are true. His attempt, therefore, is to lead them through the same process of reasoning that produced his conversion. Some may refuse to be led, and some who allow themselves to be led (including, it seems, most modern readers) may find that Descartes' arguments do not compel their assent. But Descartes' view, as I understand it, is that those who do allow themselves to be led and who fully understand the arguments of *Meditation III* will come to regard their being psychologically compelled to affirm a proposition as conclusive evidence that the proposition is in fact true.

If our being compelled to affirm a proposition does guarantee its truth, there can be nothing wrong with the "trickery" of which Descartes is sometimes accused. In presenting a psychologically compelling argument for a proposition (Descartes would say), we are in fact proving that the proposition is true. And where is the trick in that?

CHAPTER 7

Clarity and Distinctness

As I argued in Chapter 3, Descartes resolves in *Meditation I* to allow a proposition into his new system of belief if and only if he can convince the Demon's Advocate that it is true. Since the arguments of *Meditation III* and *IV* have silenced the Advocate (insofar as his position rested on his acceptance of the hypothesis of the evil demon), Descartes must establish a new criterion for a proposition's acceptability for the subsequent *Meditations*. The new criterion, which he establishes in *Meditations IV* and *V*, is clarity and distinctness. "When I limit my Will's range of judgment to the things presented clearly and distinctly to my understanding," he writes near the end of *Meditation IV*, "I obviously cannot err. . . . Whatever I clearly and distinctly grasp is unquestionably true" (AT 7:62).

In this chapter, I will examine Descartes' views on clarity and distinctness. After looking at what he means by *clarity* and *distinctness*, I will move to an examination of the process by which he tries to make ideas clear and distinct. Then, after examining his reasons for thinking that clarity and distinctness guarantee truth and certainty, I will connect Descartes' conception of clarity and distinctness to his conception of essence.

Clarity

Descartes sometimes calls the process by which we become aware of ideas in us *intuition,* a term that derives from a Latin verb, *tueor,* meaning "to look," and he often describes mental intuition in language borrowed from the vocabulary of optics. When we look at a physical object, we detect it with our eyes, provided that the conditions are right. Similarly, Descartes would say, when we intuit an idea, we detect it with our "mind's eye."

To mark some ideas off from others, Descartes uses the term *clear*—more than twenty times in *Meditation III* and almost as many times in *Meditation IV.* Yet he makes no attempt to define this term in the *Meditations.* Even in *Replies II,* where he offers formal definitions of many of the terms he uses in the *Meditations,* there is no attempt at definition of this crucial term. There is, however, this brief attempt at explanation in the *Principles:* "I call a perception clear when it is present and apparent to an attentive mind—as we say that we see things clearly when they are present to a regarding eye and act on it with sufficient strength" (*Princ. I,* 45, AT 8:21–22). Relying on the analogy to seeing, Descartes here explains what he means by clear conception simply by noting that it stands to mental seeing as clear sensory perception stands to seeing with the eyes.

Three aspects of the analogy seem obvious. First, according to Descartes, as a sentient being sees something through a special organ of sense (the eye), a cognizant being grasps truths through an "organ" of the mind (the Understanding). Second, according to Descartes, as we can turn our heads and eyes to determine which objects are in our fields of vision, we can voluntarily direct our Understandings toward one idea or another. Third, according to Descartes, as we can see things only when light is reflected from them to our eyes, we can understand things only when they are "illuminated" by an intellectual "light" (see, for example, *Med. III,* AT 7:38).

A fourth aspect of the comparison may be less obvious: While the old saying that seeing is believing may not be philosophically acceptable, seeing often does lead directly to believing. On the basis of my present visual sensations, for example, I believe that there is a table before me, a calendar on the wall, and so on. As a matter of psychological fact, I can-not by simple act of will prevent myself from believing that these things are here. Indeed, even if I have good reason for believing that my senses are deceiving me, I may find myself psychologically unable to prevent myself from holding the beliefs toward which my sensations incline me.[1] Descartes extends this thought to mental perception: in his view, as clear sensory perception inclines us toward belief, so does clear mental ap-prehension.

And there is also a fifth aspect to the analogy. Seeing with our eyes, we sometimes get things wrong. Descartes' assimilation of conception to vision therefore suggests that mistakes may be possible in the case of conception—that we might somehow misperceive the natures that are before our minds. If we "glance" carelessly at the nature of the triangle, for instance, we may mistakenly come to believe that the sum of the in-terior angles differs from one triangle to another. Nothing that we men-tally "see" truly justifies that belief, of course. But, if we aren't careful, we may form the belief anyway. It may *seem* to us (as it does to many beginning students of geometry) that the sum of triangles' interior angles differs according to the triangles' shapes. As clear sense perception can be deceptive (at least, in some cases), so can clear conception.

From the proposed analogy of conception to perception, we can therefore derive the following picture of mental clarity: We understand clearly (says Descartes) when and only when we carefully and atten-tively direct our minds' eyes (that is, our Understandings) to something brightly illuminated by a nonphysical light, and, when we do this, we are inclined—perhaps sometimes even compelled—to affirm that what we conceive is really as we conceive it to be.

Distinctness

Most often, when Descartes uses the term *clarity* in the *Medita-tions,* it appears in the technical phrase "clear and distinct," which figures into his reasoning in several important ways. Much of the argument of *Meditation IV* is directed toward the conclusion that whatever we clearly and distinctly apprehend is true, the argument for God's existence in

Meditation V rests on the premise that we can truly attribute to a thing whatever we clearly and distinctly apprehend as belonging to its essence, and the argument for dualism in *Meditation VI* rests on the premise that whatever we clearly and distinctly apprehend can be exactly as we apprehend it.

But, despite the importance of the phrase "clear and distinct" to Descartes' reasoning, he offers no explanation of distinctness in the *Meditations*—and his brief remarks about it in the *Replies* and the *Principles* leave important questions unanswered. How do we tell whether our thoughts are distinct? What exactly is it that we apprehend distinctly—ideas of things (such as the idea of the piece of wax in *Meditation II*) or propositions (as is suggested by Descartes' use of phrases of the form "clearly and distinctly apprehend that *p*") or state of affairs (as is suggested by his use of phrases of the form "clearly and distinctly conceive of *A*'s existing apart from *B*")? If we can clearly and distinctly apprehend things of more than one of these types, does the term *distinct* apply to those things in exactly the same way? When we clearly and distinctly apprehend that *p*, does it follow that *p* is true (as is suggested by the argument of *Meditation IV*), or simply that it's logically possible that *p* (as is suggested by *Meditation VI*'s formula "Whatever I clearly and distinctly apprehend can be made by God to be exactly as I apprehend it")? If Descartes has answers to these questions, he has not explicitly presented them to his readers.

Still, if we narrow our attention to expressions of the form "the distinct idea of *x*" where *x* is an entity (rather than a proposition or state of affairs), we can make some headway toward explicating Descartes' conception of distinctness. One clue is etymological: the Latin adverb *distincte* derives from the verb *distinguere*, meaning "to demarcate," and the term *distinctly* therefore implies boundary, segregation, separation, and analysis. Its opposite, *confusedly*, implies the failure to notice boundaries, the fusion of the concepts of separate entities.

Suppose that an idea *i* comes before my mind brightly illuminated by "the light of nature" and that I direct my attention squarely to that idea. Suppose that *i* is an idea of an entity *x* and that it therefore presents *x* to me—that is, that when I entertain idea *i*, *x* is present to me as an object of that idea (Chapter 5). Finally, suppose that idea *i* also presents an entity, *y,* that is distinct from *x.* According to Descartes, my idea would be clear, since it would be "present and apparent to an attentive mind"— but it would be a confused or indistinct idea of *x,* since it contained an element distinct from *x.*

In the *Principles* (and elsewhere), when Descartes discusses clear but indistinct apprehension, the confusion he has in mind is often the blurring of the boundary between the mental and the physical. In *Principles I,* 46, for example, where his explicit aim is to explain how a mental apprehension can be clear without being distinct, he notes that people in pain often form the mistaken judgment that there is "something resembling the pain in the part of the body that hurts" (AT 8:22). The perception may be "very clear," he admits. But, since the nature of pain does not contain the idea of body, the idea of pain—in most, if not all, cases—is indistinct.

"The distinct," Descartes writes in the *Principles,* "is that which is so precise and different from all other objects that it contains within itself nothing but what is clear" (*Princ. I,* 45, AT 8:22). While we might have wished for a fuller explanation, Margaret Wilson's remark that this passage is "too obscure, problematic, and in need of interpretation" to illuminate what Descartes means by *distinct* seems to me ungenerous.[2] In saying that the object of a distinct idea is "different from all other objects," Descartes is saying that the idea of a thing *x* is distinct just in case that idea presents *x* to us without presenting anything other than *x* to us.

While insisting that ideas can be clear without being distinct, Descartes denies that they can be distinct without being clear. Why? What ensures that, if I have an idea that is of *x* and nothing else, I must have directed my mental attention squarely to that idea? Descartes' primary examples of clear and distinct ideas—the ideas of mind and of body that he develops in *Meditation II*—may suggest an answer. As he begins the *Meditations,* his ideas of mind and body are confused, as are most of his other ideas. To make these ideas distinct, he must emend them: starting with an idea of *x* developed without regard for philosophical precision, he must carefully separate from that idea the ideas of everything distinct from *x.* (As I will argue later, this is exactly what he attempts to do in *Meditation II* with his idea of mind through the Cogito and his idea of body through the thought experiment about the piece of wax.) If this process of conceptual emendation requires that we place our ideas under intense scrutiny (as seems plausible), the only process by which we might acquire distinct idea would ensure that those ideas were also clear.

The Clarification of the Idea of Body

The structure of the process through which Descartes attempts to develop clear and distinct ideas is easiest to see in the thought experiment about the piece of wax in *Meditation II*. At the point in his project at which he performs this experiment, the doubts of *Meditation I* are in force, the Demon's Advocate is still accepting the dream hypothesis (as he will until the final paragraphs of *Meditation VI*), and Descartes is therefore refusing to affirm that material objects (formally) exist. Accordingly, the discussion is not about any existing body but about the idea of body. Although the ostensible aim of the discussion is to show that the mind is more easily known than the body, Descartes is here revising the prephilosophical idea of body through clarification. In *Meditation VI*, when arguing that his mind is distinct from his body, he will point back to the passages about the wax in *Meditation II* and claim that, there, he produced a "distinct idea of bodily nature" (AT 7:78).

The process of clarifying the idea of body begins with a description of a piece of wax at moment that I will call t1: the piece of wax "has just been taken from the honeycomb; it hasn't yet completely lost the taste of honey; it still smells of the flowers from which it was gathered; its color, shape, and size are obvious; it is hard, cold, and easy to touch; it makes a sound when rapped" (*Med. II,* AT 7:30). Mentioning properties associated with each of the five senses, this catalog of the wax's sensible properties seems complete; it seems, in other words, that the list contains everything that we might learn about the wax through simple application of our unaided senses.

In the next stage of the thought experiment, Descartes imagines that he has moved the wax toward a flame, and he lists its sensible properties at a moment subsequent to t1, which I will call t2: "it loses what was left of its taste; it gives up its smell; it changes color; it loses its shape;

it gets bigger; it melts; it heats up; it becomes difficult to touch; it no longer makes a sound when struck" (AT 7:30). Between $t1$ and $t2$, the wax loses each of the sensible properties that it had at $t1$: before it was sweet but now it is tasteless; before it was yellow but now it is brown; before it was cold but now it is hot; and so on.

Is this a case in which one thing persists through time rather than one in which something goes out of existence and another takes its place? Although Descartes contends in *Meditation III* that God creates everything anew at each moment, his answer here is definitely that this is not a case of replacement: "We must say that it is the same piece of wax," he writes. "No one denies it or thinks otherwise" (AT 7:30).

Descartes calls the thing that endures through time "the piece of wax"—meaning, I suggest, "the thing that was a piece of wax at time $t1$." To make it plain that this thing might change so radically that it ceased to be a piece of wax, I will give it the nondescriptive name "w."

From Descartes' lists of w's properties at $t1$ and ts (together with the thought that the lists are complete in the way that I have indicated), we can draw the following conclusion: for any particular sensible property P, there is a moment—either $t1$ or $t2$ (or both)—at which w exists without P. If we choose hardness, for example, we will find that w existed at $t2$ without hardness. If we choose softness, we will find that w existed at $t1$ without softness. (If we choose blueness, we will find that w existed at both $t1$ and $t2$ without blueness.)

Now, as I indicated in Chapter 5, Descartes recognizes a middle ground between identity and distinctness, which I have called semidistinctness: B is semidistinct from A just in case, as a matter of logic, A could exist without B but B could not exist without A. According to Descartes, what the thought experiment has shown is that our idea of w is such that, for any particular sensible property that we might attribute to w, we can consistently conceive of w's existing without that property. Yet, for any instance of a sensible property of w, we cannot conceive of that instance existing without w. Accordingly (Descartes reasons), any sensible property that w may have is semidistinct from w itself. Thus, according to Descartes, w's sensible properties stand to w as a man's coat and hat stand to the man himself: when we detect those properties by sense, we naturally but inaccurately say that we sense w, as when we see a man's coat and hat we naturally but inaccurately say that we see the man (*Med. II,* AT 7:32).

For an idea of *w* to be distinct, however, it must be the case that nothing but *w* is present in that idea. So (Descartes might say), when we conceive of *w* as something hard or soft, hot or cold, our idea of *w* must be indistinct. He therefore writes, "Let's pay careful attention, remove everything that doesn't belong to the wax, and see what's left" (AT 7:30–31). As he sees it, what is left—the distinct idea of *w*—is simply the idea of a spatial entity capable of assuming an infinite variety of shapes and sizes. He therefore concludes that the distinct idea of *w* is simply the idea of a *res extensa,* an extended thing.

Descartes' clarification of his idea of body illustrates his general method for developing clear and distinct ideas. Beginning from our ordinary idea of a thing *x,* we delete from that idea everything that we conceive of as being in any way distinct from *x,* including the ideas of things that we conceive of as semidistinct from *x.* Eventually, we will arrive at a minimal idea of *x*—an idea that would cease to be an idea of *x,* and indeed of any complete thing, if we diminished it any further. And that minimal idea is the clear and distinct idea of *x.*

Distinct Conception and Truth

Given what I have said about clarity and distinctness, one may wonder why Descartes thinks it necessary to prove that what we clearly and distinctly apprehend is true. Consider, for instance, his clear and distinct idea of body. Apparently, beginning from a prephilosophical idea of body, he develops a clear and distinct idea through what, in modern parlance, might be called philosophical analysis. This analysis, it may seem, reveals that, when we call something a body, at least part of what we mean is that the thing is extended in space. But, if *body* just means "extended thing," it's an obvious (and trivial) truth that all bodies are extended. Why would we need proof that what Descartes finds in the clear and distinct idea of body can be truly attributed to bodies themselves?

In answering, it's important to notice that, as Descartes sees it, propositions that we affirm on the basis of clear and distinct apprehen-

sion (such as "Bodies are extended") are what I have called assent com-
pellers³ (Chapter 6). In *Meditation IV,* for example, he writes this:

> I've asked for the last few days whether anything exists in the world, and I've
> noted that, from the fact that I ask this, it follows that I exist. I couldn't fail to
> judge that which I so clearly understood to be true. This wasn't because a force
> outside me compelled me to believe, but because an intense light in my Under-
> standing produced a strong inclination of my Will. (AT 7:59)

And, in *Meditation V,* he adds, "My nature is such that, when I grasp
something clearly and distinctly, I can't fail to believe it" (AT 7:69).

Still, in *Meditation I,* the hypothesis of the evil demon created
doubt concerning assent compellers—including the simple truths of
mathematics and geometry that Descartes takes as paradigmatic examples of propositions that we clearly and distinctly apprehend (see *Princ.
I,* 30, AT 8:16–17). If the hypothesis of the evil demon calls into doubt
particular propositions that we clearly and distinctly apprehend, how can
it fail to create doubt concerning the general proposition "Whatever we
clearly and distinctly apprehend is true"—especially since the general
proposition seems far less obvious than, say, "$2 + 3 = 5$"? Also, while
the hypothesis of the evil demon only challenges the proposition in an
indirect and metalogical way, it challenges the proposition "Whatever
we clearly and distinctly apprehend is true" directly (in that it implies
the negation of that proposition). So, while the proposition "Whatever
we clearly and distinctly apprehend is true" may not require proof in the
ordinary sense of that term, it does need to be rescued from the doubts
of *Meditation I.*

Not surprisingly, this rescue rests on the theology of *Meditation III.*
Before Descartes was certain that God exists, he could suspect that his
mind might be a poorly designed instrument for discerning truth and
so have doubts about the truth of what he clearly and distinctly apprehended. But, once he is certain that his mind is the product of a perfect
God, he can no longer have these doubts—or any others—concerning
assent compellers (Chapter 5). He therefore says that, after we accept his
arguments for God's existence, we are perfectly certain of the truth of everything we clearly and distinctly apprehend. "Whenever we clearly perceive something," he writes in the *Principles,* "we spontaneously assent to
it and cannot in any way doubt that it is true" (*Principles I,* 43, AT 8:21).

And in *Meditation IV* he writes, "When I limit my will's range of judgment to the things presented clearly and distinctly to my understanding, I obviously cannot err" (AT 7:62).

As I suggested in the last section, the means by which Descartes attempts to make his ideas clear and distinct is psychological: beginning with a full, unanalyzed idea of an object *x,* he removes everything that he can from that idea without its seeming to him that he is no longer thinking of *x.* As I indicated in Chapter 6, the process by which his Understanding compels his Will to affirm propositions is also psychological. But, according to Descartes, the psychological and the epistemological converge in cases of clear and distinct perception, tied together by the theology of *Meditation III.* The psychological fact that we cannot have any doubts about the truth of what we clearly and distinctly apprehend itself proves that what we clearly and distinctly apprehend is true—because God, who designed us and who re-creates us moment by moment, would not allow a psychological mechanism that He had designed to force us to believe propositions that were in fact false.

Descartes also has a somewhat different reason for believing that whatever he clearly and distinctly apprehends is true—a reason that he indicates in passages like this one, from the end of *Meditation IV:* "Everything that I clearly and distinctly grasp is something and hence must come, not from nothing, but from God—God, I say, who is supremely perfect and who cannot possibly deceive. Therefore, what I clearly and distinctly grasp is unquestionably true" (AT 7:62). Here, where Descartes takes himself to be reviewing the main argument of *Meditation IV,* there is no mention of the design of his mind or the reliability of his psychological inclinations. Instead, the argument rests on the character of what it is that comes before his mind in clear and distinct apprehension.

As I explained in Chapter 5, Descartes posits "natures," which can be manifest in one way (formally) in the spatiotemporal order and in a very different way (namely, objectively) in our ideas. On his view, for instance, the nature of the sun manifests in the spatiotemporal order as the sun in the sky and before our minds as the sun as object of thought. Yet, as I have explained, there is a point to saying that, according to his theory, the mental entity and the physical entity are one and the same thing: both are the same nature, which is present in one way in the idea and in another way in the astronomical body.

In arguing for God's existence in *Meditation III,* Descartes makes it clear that he thinks that these natures require causes, even if they are not manifest in the spatiotemporal order. And he also asserts that the natures before his mind when he perceives something clearly and distinctly "must come, not from nothing, but from God." Accordingly, he reasons that whatever we can "read off" from clear and distinct ideas must be true. Viewing the indistinct idea of pain, we might be led to affirm the false proposition that pains have spatial location; indistinct ideas lack clarity, and God is only the cause of what is present, not of lacks. But, according to Descartes, when we view the clear and distinct idea of the triangle and notice that its interior angles equal two right angles, what we see must be true. To deny this (he would say) is to embrace the absurd view that a perfect God has deceived us by creating misleading natures and allowing those natures to come before our minds.

But why suppose that the natures that come before our minds in clear and distinct perception *are* God's products? Descartes addresses this question in *Meditation V:*

Suppose . . . that I have a mental image of a triangle. While it may be that no figure of this sort does exist or ever has existed outside my thought, the figure has a fixed nature (essence or form), immutable and eternal, which hasn't been produced by me and isn't dependent on my mind. The proof is that I can demonstrate various propositions about the triangle, such as that its angles equal two right angles and that its greatest side subtends its greatest angle. Even though I didn't think of these propositions at all when I first imagined the triangle, I now clearly see their truth whether I want to or not, and it follows that I didn't make them up. (AT 7:64)

While the details of this reasoning may be obscure, its general line seems clear: A novice geometer might make a random list of propositions about triangles that includes, say, "The interior angles of a triangle equal two right angles" and "The triangle's largest side is opposed to its smallest angle." Even if the geometer didn't initially know which of these propositions to affirm or which to deny, and even if there were no triangular objects in the world, something—the nature of the triangle, Descartes would say—would make it the case that the first of these propositions is true and the second false. This nature could not be anything that the geometer himself produced; in proving the true propositions and refuting the false, the geometer does not invent or create, but discovers what would have been the case if he or she had never existed. Indeed, since the geometer's theorems about the triangle would be true regardless of what contingencies may obtain in the world, the nature of the triangle must be something "eternal and immutable." And, as Descartes sees it, the only possible cause for an entity of this sort is God.

According to Descartes, then, if the "eternal and immutable" nature of the triangle were to come clearly and distinctly before our minds, whatever we were to read off from that nature must be true. Since our perception of the nature is clear and distinct, we would not be to blame for false beliefs acquired in this way. The whole blame would fall on God, who is responsible both for the design of our minds and for the characteristics of the eternal and immutable natures that come before our minds. But God (Descartes reasons) is morally perfect and hence entirely blameless.

Essence

To make the idea of x clear and distinct, I have argued, one must delete from that idea everything we conceive of as being in any way distinct from x, including the ideas of things semidistinct from x. But according to Descartes, everything that we clearly and distinctly apprehend is true. Consequently, he writes in *Meditation V* that "anything whose idea I can draw from my thought must in fact have everything that I clearly and distinctly grasp it to have" (AT 7:65). Similarly, in *Replies II*, he writes, "To say that something is contained in the nature or concept of a thing [*in natura sive conceptu*] is just to say that it is true of that thing and can be affirmed of it" (AT 7:162). By appealing to this principle, he can move, for example, from the observation that he clearly and distinctly conceives of the physical object w as an extended thing to the conclusion that w is extended.

And there is a stronger principle that Descartes uses in his reasoning. If our clear and distinct idea of x contains the idea of the property

P (he claims), we can be certain, not just that x happens to have P, but that x *necessarily* has P—that the proposition "x has P" is an eternal truth. Believing that for each object x there will be at least one property present in the clear and distinct idea of x, he therefore infers that there will be at least one property such that x must have P at every moment at which x exists.

Descartes posits several attributes, such as duration (*Princ. I*, 62, AT 8:31), that are of this sort. But he also says (in the *Principles*, not in the *Meditations*) that, for each object x, there will be exactly one attribute that every other property of x presupposes. As he sees it, we cannot conceive of an entity clearly and distinctly without conceiving of this attribute—which he calls the entity's "essence, principle property, or nature" (*Princ. I*, 52–53, AT 8:24–25).

In the case of the piece of wax, the principle property is of course spatial extension. While we can conceive that w (the thing that was a piece of wax at t1) might change into a bronze statue, a boulder, or even a planet, we cannot even conceive of w's becoming something other than an object extended in space. So, according to Descartes, the clear and distinct idea of w is not the idea of bare substratum or propertyless created substance, but the idea of something with the attribute of spatial extension. Since the same can be said of any body whatever, he concludes that the essence of a body is extension (*Princ. I*, 53, AT 8:25; *Meditation VI*, AT 7:78).

But what exactly does this mean? Is the essence of w the general property of extension? Or is the essence of w the particular manifestation of extension found in w—that is, w's extension?

Descartes titles *Meditation V* "On the Essence of Material Objects . . . ," and he writes in *Meditation VI* about "identifying the essence [rather than the essence*s*] of physical objects" (AT 7:83). From these passages, it seems that, in Descartes' view, all bodies have the same essence: the attribute of extension.

There is, however, a problem with this suggestion. In the *Principles*, where Descartes directs his attention directly to such matters, he seems to say that an object is, strictly speaking, identical to its essence. He writes, for instance, that, if we are unable to form a clear and distinct idea of a substance without conceiving of it as having a certain attribute, the distinction between that substance and that attribute is merely a "distinction of thought" (*Princ. I, 62*, AT 8:30). And in the French version of the *Principles*, he adds that "generally, all the attributes that cause us to have diverse thoughts of the same thing, such as the extension of body and [body's] property of divisibility, do not differ from the body which is to us the [object in which they reside], or the one from the other, excepting so far as we sometimes think confusedly of the one without the other."[4] Apparently, Descartes' considered opinion was that our distinction of an object from its essence is the product of confusion and that it has no grounding in the world outside our thoughts. (If he did hold this view, we can make sense of his saying that every property of an object depends on that object's essence or principle property. If the essence of a thing *x* is *x* itself, doesn't it follow that everything that derives its existence from *x* depends on *x*'s essence?)

If an object is identical to its essence, however, it seems that the essence of *w* could not be the general property of extension. While it seems plausible that *w* could not possibly exist without the general property of extension, it seems obvious that the general property of extension might manifest itself (formally) in a world in which *w* did not exist—a world lacking *w* but containing other physical objects. But, according to Descartes' theory, the criterion of numerical identity is the impossibility of separate existence: as he sees it, *A* and *B* are numerically identical just in case *A* cannot possibly exist without *B* and *B* cannot possibly exist without *A*. So Descartes seems committed to the view that the general property of extension is not identical to *w* itself.

Descartes might avoid this problem by saying that *w*'s essence is extension as manifest in *w*—that is, *w*'s extension rather than the general property of extension. On his view, *w* could not possibly exist without its essence, and it seems clear that *w*'s extension could not possibly exist without *w* itself. Accordingly, if *w*'s essence were *w*'s extension, it would seem to follow that *w* and its essence do satisfy Descartes' criterion for identity. It might be possible to conceive of this one entity in two different ways and so to draw a merely "conceptual distinction" (Descartes might say), but such a distinction would not correspond to a distinction in the world, or even to the relation of semidistinctness.

But, on the face of it, the view that *w* is identical to its essence seems implausible. Apparently, while w is extended, w's extension is not itself extended—and how could something that is extended be identical to something that isn't? More important, while w is an extended thing, w's extension is a property or attribute, not a *thing* at all. But, if w and w's extension do not even belong to the same ontological category, does it make sense to say that the only distinction between them is purely conceptual? Wouldn't the claim that w is identical to w's extension imply that something was one step down from itself?[5]

It may be that Descartes has answers to these questions—that his system of ontological concepts allows him to explain how something with one degree of reality can be only conceptually distinct from something at another. Still, it seems to me a criticism of Descartes' reasoning, in both the *Meditations* and the *Principles,* that he does not provide us with such an explanation.

CHAPTER 8

God's Essence and Existence

"If anything whose idea I can draw from my thought must in fact have everything that I clearly and distinctly grasp it to have," Descartes asks rhetorically in *Meditation V,* "can't I derive from this a proof of God's existence?" Then, having already offered two arguments for God's existence in *Meditation III,* he constructs another.

In this chapter, I will examine this new argument. After explicating the argument's reasoning, I will consider several objections and Descartes' replies. One of the objections will be that the reasoning is circular: having based the validation of clear and distinct apprehension on the premise that God exists, Descartes seems to rest his new argument for God's existence on the premise that clear and distinct apprehension is reliable. The discussion of this objection will lead back to a consideration of Descartes' general strategy in the *Meditations.*

The Structure of Descartes' Ontological Argument

Descartes' most succinct summary of *Meditation V*'s primary argument for God's existence is perhaps in *Replies I:* "That which we clearly and distinctly understand to pertain to the true and immutable nature, essence, or form of a thing can be truly affirmed of that thing. But, once we have investigated what God is with sufficient care, we clearly and distinctly understand that it pertains to His true and immutable nature that he exists. Therefore, we can now truly affirm of God that He exists" (AT 7:115–16). In outline, the argument is this:

8.1. Whatever we clearly and distinctly understand to belong to the essence of a thing can truly be affirmed of that thing.

8.2. We clearly and distinctly understand that existence belongs to the essence of God.

8.3. Therefore, we can truly affirm existence of God—that is, God exists.

Various formulations of this reasoning appear elsewhere in Descartes' writings—notably in *Meditation V* (AT 7:65–66).[1]

The argument's starting point—premise 8.1—is a corollary to Descartes' contention (discussed in the previous chapter) that whatever we clearly and distinctly apprehend is true. To make the idea of an object *x* clear and distinct, we remove from that idea everything that we conceive of as distinct from *x*, leaving only what Descartes calls that thing's true and immutable nature or essence. As he sees it, when we view such a nature, we find ourselves psychologically unable to prevent ourselves from attributing whatever is in it to *x*. (When we have a clear and distinct idea of the triangle, for example, we find ourselves compelled to affirm that the triangle has three sides and three angles.) Since he takes himself to have shown that both that his mind and the natures that come before that mind are the product of a veracious God, he concludes that whatever can be found in the clear and distinct idea of *x* can truly be attributed to *x*. Indeed, as he sees it, whatever can be found in the clear and distinct idea of *x* is part of *x*'s nature or essence—a collection of attributes that are somehow constitutive of *x* (Chapter 7).

But, even if we grant all of this, isn't there a problem with premise 8.1? Descartes admits that we have clear and distinct ideas of things that do not (formally) exist. He develops a clear and distinct idea of body in *Meditations II* and *V*, for example, although he does not attempt to establish the formal existence of bodies until *Meditation VI*. But what sense does it make to say that we can truly attribute a property to an object *x* if *x* doesn't exist? If *x* doesn't exist, it seems, there is nothing there to bear the attribution. (Perhaps Gassendi points to an objection of this sort when, in *Objections V,* he asks Descartes, "When Plato no longer exists, where is his essence?" [AT 7:324].)

Here it's important to recall that, since *Meditation III,* Descartes has supposed that (even if they don't exist formally) the things of which we have ideas exist as objects of ideas and that a sentence of the form "*x* has property *P*" may be true even if *x*'s existence is of this kind. For example, according to Descartes, from the observation that the clear and distinct idea of the triangle contains the idea of three-sidedness, we can infer that the nature or essence of the triangle contains three-sidedness and hence that the proposition "The triangle has three sides" is true— regardless of whether there are any triangular things in spatiotemporal order. Similarly, he reasons, if we perceive that a property *P* belongs to God's essence, we can truly say, "God has *P*"—even if we do not know whether God's reality goes beyond existence as the object of an idea.

But why accept the argument's second premise, 8.2—that we clearly and distinctly apprehend that existence belongs to God's essence? Descartes acknowledges that this is a difficult question to answer persuasively. "Since I'm accustomed to distinguishing existence from essence in other cases," he writes, "I find it easy to convince myself that I can separate God's existence from His essence" (AT 7:66). Yet, in this case (he says), such a separation would be a mistake: "It's clear that I can no more separate God's existence from His essence than a triangle's angles equaling two right angles from the essence of the triangle, or the idea of a valley from the idea of a mountain" (*Med. V,* AT 7:66).

In *Meditation V,* Descartes' argument for this point rests on the idea of perfection. "It's no less impossible to think that God (the supremely perfect being) lacks existence (a perfection) than to think that a mountain lacks a valley," he writes (AT 7:66). But why suppose that the idea of the primary substance that Descartes calls God is the idea of something possessing all perfections? And why suppose that existence is a perfection—rather than, as Gassendi insists, something without which a thing cannot have any perfections? (*Obj. V,* AT 7:323). Since Descartes does not even try to address such issues in the *Meditations,* his talk about perfections serves to multiply, rather than settle, questions about the soundness of his reasoning.

But perhaps Descartes could have made his point here without appeal to any thesis about perfections. As I've said, his idea of God is the idea of "a [primary] substance that is infinite, independent, supremely intelligent, and supremely powerful—the thing from which I and everything else that may exist derive our existence" (AT 7:45). This idea, he repeatedly insists, is clear and distinct: he has paid attention to it and deleted from it everything that he conceives of as being distinct from God, including the ideas of things that are semidistinct from Him. But, according to Descartes, whatever remains in the idea of *x* once that idea has been made clear and distinct is part of *x*'s nature or essence. Accordingly (Descartes might reason), since the idea of substance is the idea of something that grounds its own existence, it must follow from God's essence that He brings himself into (formal) existence at every moment. While admitting that we can fully grasp the essence of the triangle without attributing (formal) existence to triangles, Descartes might therefore maintain that we cannot grasp the essence of God without attributing existence to Him. God is primary substance, he claims, and the essence of substance is (self-caused) existence at every moment.

To some, this line of argument seems more Spinozistic than Cartesian. Yet, when Descartes attempts to define the term *God* (for instance, in *Meditation III* [AT 7:45] or in *Replies II* [AT 7:162]), he says that God is an unbounded primary substance—something whose nature ensures its existence. Even Descartes' troublesome talk about perfections can be understood in these terms: to say that God has all perfection is to say that everything positive that can be said can truly be attributed to Him in the highest degree, and the most positive thing that can be said about an entity is that it exists independently of others—or, in other words, that it is primary substance.

Granted that the idea of God is the idea of substance and that it pertains to the essence of substance to exist, Descartes concludes that God exists. Indeed, since the clear and distinct idea of substance is the idea of something that brings itself into existence at every moment, Descartes concludes that God "has necessarily existed from all eternity and will continue to exist into eternity" (*Med. V,* AT 7:68).

Caterus' Objection

One of the best-known objections to *Meditation V*'s argument for God's existence is developed by Caterus, who asks us to consider the following argument:

8.1. Whatever we clearly and distinctly understand to belong to the essence of a thing *x* can be truly affirmed of *x*.

8.2'. We clearly and distinctly understand that existence belongs to the essence of the existing lion.

8.3'. Therefore, we can truly affirm existence of the existing lion—that is, the existing lion exists.

According to Caterus, God must always have had a clear and distinct idea of the compound *existing lion*—an idea that contains the idea of existence as well as that of lionhood. "Isn't it the case," Caterus asks, "that the idea of this composite, insofar as it is composite, involves both of its elements essentially? That is, isn't existence involved in the essence of the composite existing lion?" (*Obj. I*, AT 7:99). Believing that the answer is yes, Caterus asserts 8.2'. The argument's only other premise, 8.1, is the initial premise of *Meditation V*'s argument for God's existence. But Caterus correctly contends that the argument from 8.1 and 8.2' to 8.3' is unacceptable; if it were sound, we could begin from the idea of anything *x*, annex to that idea the idea of existence (producing the idea of the existing *x*), construct an argument like that about the existing lion, and show that the existing *x* exists. Therefore, without any analysis of what goes wrong in Descartes' reasoning, Caterus concludes that *Meditation V*'s argument for God's existence must also be unacceptable.

According to Descartes, however, the argument from 8.1 and 8.2' to 8.3' differs importantly from *Meditation V*'s argument for God's existence. Simply put, Descartes' contention is that, while 8.2 ("We clearly and distinctly understand that existence belongs to the essence of the God") is true, 8.2' ("We clearly and distinctly understand that existence belongs to the essence of the existing lion") is not.

Imagine that we have found a particular existing lion—say, Leo—that we have formed an idea of Leo, and that we want to make that idea clear and distinct. To sidestep unnecessary complexity, let's accept

Descartes' view that nonhuman animals, such as Leo, are mere automata. Then our model for developing a clear and distinct idea of Leo might be Descartes' thought experiment in *Meditation II* about the piece of wax. We can imagine that, as we bring Leo near a fire, his color changes, his smell changes, the sound he emits changes, and so on. Since we can imagine the thing that is Leo enduring such changes, we can conclude that his sensible qualities, such as color, are merely modes of Leo himself, and we can therefore delete the ideas of those qualities from our idea of him. When we are done with the deletions, Descartes would say, we will find that the clear and distinct idea of Leo (*qua* physical object) is exactly the same as the clear and distinct idea of the piece of wax: the idea of an extended thing. But, as I have explained, Descartes held that what remains in the idea of *x* after we have made that idea clear and distinct is the essence of *x*. So, according to Descartes, extension is the essence Leo, as it is of all physical objects.

In *Meditation V,* Descartes expresses his belief that, besides physical objects, there are abstract entities such as the Triangle:

I find in myself innumerable ideas of things which, though they may not exist outside me, can't be said to be nothing. While I have some control over my thoughts of these things, I do not make the things up: they have their own real and immutable natures. Suppose, for example, that I have a mental image of a triangle. While it may be that no figure of this sort does exist or ever has existed outside my thought, the figure has a fixed nature (essence or form), immutable and eternal, which hasn't been produced by me and isn't dependent on my mind. (AT 7:66)

In saying that such abstract entities "can't be said to be nothing," he implies that there is some sense of *exist* in which we can truly say that they exist. And, although he himself disdains appeals to ordinary ways of speaking, such an appeal might support his point here. We naturally say that there *is* a plane, closed figure (namely, the Triangle) that has exactly three sides and that there *is* an integer (namely, three) between two and four.

As the Triangle stands to triangular physical objects (we might assume), the Lion stands to particular lions, such as Leo. And, as the Triangle has an essence other than extension (namely, three-sidedness), the Lion has an essence other than extension. While Descartes says in his reply to Caterus that we have not yet clearly ascertained what this essence is (AT 7:117), he does not deny that there is such an essence or that it is possible for us to discover it. But presumably, discovering the essence of the Lion would not reveal whether there are lions in the spatiotemporal order, any more than discovering the essence of the Triangle reveals whether there are any triangular physical objects.

But what about the essence of the compound *the existing lion*? As Caterus admits, the idea of this compound is one that we ourselves have fabricated. And, according to Descartes, since we have put the idea together, we can analyze it by "dividing" it into its elements (AT 7:117). But an idea that can be divided in this way is not clear and distinct; while an idea that can be divided can be diminished, a distinct idea is one from which everything that can be subtracted *has* been subtracted. Descartes' views on clarity and distinctness therefore entail that there is no clear and distinct idea of the existing lion.

Conjoined to the epistemological position for which Descartes argues in *Meditation IV,* the claim that we cannot have a clear and distinct idea of the existing lion has an important consequence. If an idea is clear and distinct, says Descartes, we can be sure that the idea presents something, if only a nature. "When I limit my will's range of judgment to the things presented clearly and distinctly to my understanding, I obviously cannot err," he writes in *Meditation IV,* "for everything that I clearly and distinctly grasp is something and hence must come, not from nothing, but from God—God, I say, who is supremely perfect and who cannot possibly deceive" (AT 7:62). On the other hand, if an idea is not clear and distinct, Descartes refuses to say that it presents an immutable nature. Thus, in his reply to Caterus, he writes, "When I think of a winged horse, or an actually existing lion, or a triangle inscribed in a square, I easily see that I can also think of a horse without wings, of a lion that doesn't exist, or of a triangle without a square, and so on, and therefore that these things do not have true and immutable natures" (AT 7:117). According to Descartes, then, while God's veracity ensures that a clear and distinct idea presents a true and immutable nature to us, there is no guarantee that an indistinct idea presents anything to us other than a "fictitious nature composed by our own Understandings" (AT 7:117).

On Descartes' view, when we say something true about the Triangle (such as that its interior angles equal two right angles), what we say is made true by the Triangle's true and immutable nature. Similarly, as he sees it, if we could say something true about the existing lion, what we said would be made true by the true and immutable nature of the existing lion. But for reasons that I have outlined, he doesn't believe that the compound *the existing lion* has a true and immutable nature.

When we focus on the similarity of the sentence "The triangle is a polygon" to the sentence "The existing lion is of the genus *Panthera*," it may seem odd for Descartes to accept the first but not the second, but is his view on the matter really counterintuitive? It is a demonstrable fact that (in some sense of *is*) there is a plain closed figure with three sides (the Triangle), and, as Descartes notes, in proving theorems about the Triangle, mathematicians (sometimes) take themselves to be making discoveries about this thing. In contrast, zoologists are more likely to take the sentence "The existing lion is of the genus *Panthera*" to be about particular lions (or perhaps about the Lion) than about a compound abstract entity that might be called the Existing Lion.

Granted his views about clear and distinct ideas and about abstract entities, Descartes can therefore point to several differences between 8.2′ ("We clearly and distinctly understand that existence belongs to the true and immutable nature or essence of the existing lion") and 8.2 ("We clearly and distinctly understand that existence belongs to the true and immutable nature or essence of God"). As he sees it, we cannot have a clear and distinct idea of the existing lion, there is nothing that we might call the true and immutable nature of the Existing Lion, and we therefore cannot attribute anything to an abstract called the Existing Lion (because there is nothing in the world to bear that attribution). In contrast, on his view, we do have a clear and distinct idea of God, there is a true and immutable nature of God, and we therefore can attribute properties to God without assuming that He formally exists.

Arnauld's Objection

At root, what is wrong with Caterus' objection is that he fails to understand what Descartes means by "clear and distinct" and therefore leaps to the (false) conclusion that we have a clear and distinct idea of the existing lion. But doesn't the acknowledgment that Descartes' argument rests his conception of clarity and distinctness open the door to another objection? Consider, for instance, this passage from Arnauld's *Objections:* "How can [Descartes] avoid reasoning in a circle when he says that we are sure that what we clearly and distinctly perceive is true only because God exists? Since we can be sure that God exists only because we clearly and distinctly perceive that He does, we ought to be sure that what we clearly and distinctly perceive is true before we are sure that God exists" (AT 7:214). Arnauld seems to think that Descartes has committed himself to both of these propositions:

8.4. We must be sure that God exists before we can be sure that what we clearly and distinctly perceive is true.

8.5. We must be sure that what we clearly and distinctly perceive is true before we can be sure that God exists.

Descartes seems committed to 8.4; to become perfectly certain that what we clearly and distinctly apprehend is true, he says, we must conclusively rule out the hypothesis of the evil demon by becoming certain that there is a veracious God. He also seems committed to 8.5: "If I were ignorant of God," he writes in *Meditation V,* "I might come to doubt [the] truth [of various propositions] as soon as my mind's eye turned away from [their] demonstration[s], even if I recalled having once grasped [them] clearly" (AT 7:69–70). While 8.4 and 8.5 are not strictly inconsistent, they do seem inconsistent with Descartes' claim to have moved in *Meditations III* and *IV* from doubt to perfect certainty. If we cannot possibly do a first thing until we have done a second and cannot possibly do the second until we have done the first, it seems to follow that we can never do either.

In reply to Arnauld, Descartes writes this:

I have already explained this point satisfactorily . . . by distinguishing that which I clearly and distinctly perceive from that which I remember having clearly perceived in the past. At first, we are sure that God exists because we attend to the proofs for his existence. Later, it is enough for us to remember that we clearly perceived something in order for us to be certain that it is true—but this is enough only because we know that God exists and does not deceive. (*Replies IV,* AT 7:245–46)

As I understand it, Descartes here admits that 8.5 is true—but only when qualified. As he sees it, we must be sure that whatever we clearly and distinctly perceive is true before we can be sure that God exists *if* we no longer have convincing arguments for God's existence before our minds. As I argued in Chapter 5, Descartes believes that, when we keep the arguments of *Meditation III* in mind, we cannot prevent ourselves from affirming "God exists" and that we therefore cannot have any doubts at all about that proposition's truth. Still, according to Descartes, when his attention to such arguments has flagged or he has forgotten the arguments altogether, his Understanding may no longer compel his Will to affirm that God exists, the hypothesis of the evil demon may again seem to him to make sense, and he may again have grounds for doubt concerning God's existence. So, even though he becomes perfectly certain that God exists in *Meditation III,* he has not achieved the stability of belief that was his aim. The possibility still exists that, as a result of inattention or failure of memory, he may come to doubt, or even to reject, the propositions that he once established with perfect certainty.

Descartes infers "Everything that I have ever clearly and distinctly apprehended is true" from "God exists" to close this remaining opening for doubt. In *Meditation V,* he writes,

> Now I grasp that God exists, and I understand both that everything else depends on Him and that He's not a deceiver. From this, I infer that everything I clearly and distinctly grasp must be true. Even if I no longer pay attention to the grounds on which I judged God to exist, my recollection that I once clearly and distinctly knew Him to exist ensures that no contrary ground can be produced to push me toward doubt. About God's existence, I have true and certain knowledge. (AT 7:70)

When geometers use a theorem, they are not expected to have its proof in mind. It's enough that they remember once having proven it (and, perhaps, that they can produce the proof if pressed). Similarly, after Descartes has established that what he clearly and distinctly apprehends is true, he feels free to assert propositions—such as "God exists"—that he remembers having clearly and distinctly apprehended, even if he does not have their proofs in mind at the moment.

In effect, having constructed two arguments for God's existence in

Meditation III, Descartes goes on in *Meditation V* to construct another argument to the same conclusion: "Whatever I have ever clearly and distinctly apprehended is true; I once clearly and distinctly apprehended that God exists; therefore, God exists." Superficially, this argument resembles the argument from 8.1 and 8.2 to 8.3 in that each moves from a general principle about the reliability of clear and distinct perception to the conclusion that God exists.

Now, as Arnauld notes in his objection, Descartes contends that we cannot be perfectly certain of what we clearly and distinctly apprehend until we are certain that God exists. Until then, we should have some suspicion that the hypothesis of the evil demon might be true, and this suspicion should provides us with grounds for doubt concerning even what we grasp clearly and distinctly. As I have explained, Descartes also believes that, when we have the arguments of *Meditation III* in mind, we are perfectly certain that God exists; at these moments, nothing anyone could say to us would make it reasonable for us to abandon the belief that God exists (Chapter 6). Yet this certainty may not be permanent; as the project of the *Meditations* continues, we may lose sight of the reasoning of *Meditations III* and *IV,* and the proposition "God exists" may slide back into doubt. So, contrary to Arnauld's suggestion, Descartes can consistently maintain both that we can be perfectly certain of what we clearly and distinctly apprehend only after we have proven that God exists and that (after ceasing to pay attention to the arguments of *Meditation III*) we can be certain that God exists only after we have demonstrated that whatever we have once clearly and distinctly apprehended is true.

Still, the objection forces Descartes to reveal how far he has moved (perhaps intentionally) from his original project. In *Meditation I,* the primary rule of the project was "Assert a proposition only if you can convince the Demon's Advocate of its truth." In *Meditation IV,* after the Demon's Advocate was forced to abandon the hypothesis of the evil demon, the rule became "Assert only what you clearly and distinctly apprehend." Yet, in *Meditation V,* Descartes asserts a premise—namely, "I once clearly and distinctly apprehended that God exists"—whose truth he does not clearly and distinctly apprehend. His only evidence for this premise is what he remembers, and, even in cases of this sort, memory is notoriously unreliable. Geometers, logicians, and others who construct formal systems sometimes sincerely and confidently report that they recall having proved a theorem when they have not done so. So, there is a hypothesis—namely, that Descartes misremembers having clearly and distinctly apprehended that God exists—which he should suspect to be true (even after *Meditation IV*) and which he should view as challenging his beliefs about what he once clearly and distinctly apprehended.

It may be that, by the middle of *Meditation V,* Descartes has given up on the project of achieving perfect certainty. As I argued in Chapter 2, his reason for seeking perfect certainty is that he wants to establish a system of beliefs that is stable—immune to upheaval of the sort that occurred in the Scientific Revolution. But, in *Meditation V,* he seems to face a choice between certainty and stability: he can continue to subscribe to the rule "Assert only those propositions of whose truth you are perfectly certain," or he can stabilize his system of beliefs by allowing himself to assert propositions that he remembers once having perceived clearly and distinctly. Since he originally sought perfect certainty as a means to stability rather than as an end in itself (Chapter 2), it would not be surprising for him to choose stability.

Another Round with a Cartesian Circle

In the last section, I argued that Descartes' distinction of what we now clearly and distinctly apprehend from what we remember once having clearly and distinctly apprehended answers Arnauld's objection of circularity. But there are other, more obvious objections along the same lines.

In *Meditation III,* Descartes offers two arguments to the conclusion "God exists." In *Meditation IV,* he uses "God exists" as a premise for an argument to the conclusion that whatever he clearly and distinctly apprehends is true. Then, in *Meditation V,* he argues from "Everything that I clearly and distinctly apprehend is true" to the conclusion "God exists." That there is a loop is undeniable. And the point made in reply to Arnauld—that what we recall having clearly and distinctly apprehended must be true—does not seem relevant here. As Alan Gewirth writes,

"The central argument of Descartes' metaphysics proceeds through clear and distinct ideas to the veracity of God, and then from God's veracity to the truth of clear and distinct perceptions."[2]

If Descartes has a defense against this charge, it must be that this loop is not objectionable. We might therefore approach his defense by asking what is generally objectionable about circular reasoning. In the most blatant cases—when someone offers an argument of the form "*p* ; therefore, *p*"—the reasoning is valid; there is no possibility that the premise of such an argument might be true while its conclusion is false. Indeed, if "*p*" is in fact true, the argument "*p* ; therefore *p*" is sound. Then why is circular reasoning *ever* objectionable?

The answer has to do with the typical use of argument: to convince. In typical cases, person *A* calls person *B*'s attention to propositions that *B* already believes (premises) in the attempt to get *B* to affirm another proposition (a conclusion). In such cases, if *B* believes the conclusion before *A* begins, *A*'s interaction with *B* will be pointless. Why labor to convince someone of something that he or she already believes? On the other hand, if *B* does not accept the premises of *A*'s argument, *B* will find *A*'s argument unconvincing. So, in typical cases, if the conclusion of *A*'s argument is among its premises, or if *B* believes the premises of *A*'s argument only because he or she has derived it from the proposition that is the conclusion of *A*'s argument, *A*'s argument will be either pointless or unconvincing.

But *does* Descartes construct *Meditation V*'s argument for God's existence—that is, the argument from 8.1 and 8.2 to 8.3—to *convince* himself, or anyone else, that God exists? In answering, it may help to notice that, as I have been interpreting it, the program of the *Meditations* has two distinct stages.

In the first stage, which begins in *Meditation I*, Descartes follows one basic rule: "Affirm a proposition only if the Demon's Advocate can be brought to believe that it is true." While his overriding aim in the *Meditations* is to develop a perfectly "firm and stable" system of beliefs, the specific aims of this first stage are to settle the doubts of *Meditation I* and to find a method by which to acquire beliefs not subject to those (or any other) doubts. This stage of the project ends in *Meditation IV* with the establishment of the rule of clarity and distinctness: "Affirm only what you clearly and distinctly understand."

The second stage of Descartes' project begins in *Meditation V* and continues into *Meditation VI*. Here the aim is to apply the method established in the first stage to the development of a system of beliefs. In the second stage, having developed and validated a method, Descartes puts that method to use.

Granted this division of the *Meditations'* project, Descartes might say that his intention in constructing *Meditation V*'s argument for God's existence is not to convince anyone that God exists, but to show that the proposition "God exists" satisfies his new criterion of acceptability—the criterion of clarity and distinctness. In constructing the proof (he might go on), he is like a geometer who, fully convinced of the truth of an obvious proposition, constructs a proof for it anyway—not to convince anyone that the proposition is true, but to demonstrate that it satisfies the formal criterion of derivability.

The arguments for God's existence in *Meditation III* are important to Descartes' program; he uses them to settle many of the doubts of *Meditation I,* to silence the Demon's Advocate, and to establish the rule of clarity and distinctness. Still, even though he finds *Meditation III*'s arguments compelling, and even though they rid him of all doubt concerning God's existence, they do not serve his purposes in *Meditation V.* He explicitly argues, after all, that, if he affirms what he does not clearly and distinctly apprehend, he has committed an error even if the proposition that he affirms is true.

If I suspend judgment when I don't clearly and distinctly grasp what is true, I obviously do right and am not deceived. But, if I either affirm or deny in a case of this sort, I misuse my freedom of choice. If I affirm what is false, I clearly err, and, if I stumble onto the truth, I'm still blameworthy, since the light of nature reveals that a perception of the Understanding should always precede a decision of the Will. (AT 7:59–60)

But *Meditation III*'s arguments do not themselves rest on a clear and distinct conception of God's nature. (As Descartes tells us in *Replies II,* the intended audience for these arguments includes those who have not yet developed a "clear mental vision" [AT 7:168].) So, whatever their merits and importance to Descartes' program, the arguments of *Meditation III* cannot fully justify his accepting the proposition "God exists" into his system. Since his criterion of acceptability is clear and distinct apprehension, only an argument based on such an apprehension of God's nature—such as one from 8.1 and 8.2 to 8.3—will do.

If this interpretation is right, it explains why, in a prefatory letter to the *Meditations,* Descartes says that his two main purposes are to establish the existence of God and the immortality of the soul (AT 7:1–2), completely ignoring such propositions as "I exist" and "Whatever I clearly and distinctly perceive is true" that he labors to establish in *Meditations II* through *IV.* While such propositions obviously do play important roles in the program of the *Meditations,* their place is in the discussion of method. Descartes begins the development of his "firm and stable" system of beliefs in *Meditation V after* he has solved these problems. And the two primary propositions that he establishes after that are those that he mentions in his prefatory letter—namely, that God exists (*Meditation V*) and that his mind is distinct from his body (*Meditation VI*).

Finally, as I have argued, the interpretation of Descartes' strategy that I have offered explains why Descartes, who validates clear and distinct apprehension on the grounds that God exists in *Meditation IV,* goes on in *Meditation V* to use the proposition "Whatever I clearly and distinctly perceive is true" as a premise of an argument for God's existence. On the interpretation I have offered, he offers the argument of *Meditation V,* not to convince anyone of the truth of its conclusion, but to show that the proposition "God exists" meets the standard that he himself has established for acceptability: the standard of clear and distinct perception. As far as I can see, there is nothing objectionable about this.

CHAPTER 9

Mind and Body

Modern materialists as well as spokesmen for the New Age sometimes blame Descartes for inventing the doctrine that mind is distinct from body, but in a letter prefatory to the *Meditations* Descartes tells us that his aim is to demonstrate the truth of the *traditional* view that the soul survives the death of the body (AT 7:1–6)[1]—a view that is deeply embedded in Christianity and that dates back (at least) to ancient Egypt. Also, in arguing for this view, Descartes turns his back on the then current position that, being images of a triune God, we have *three* parts: a mind, a soul, and a body. And, although Descartes did believe that the thing that thinks his thoughts could exist in separation from his body, he says that a human being is a union of a body and soul. To some extent, the movement in *Meditation VI* is therefore toward integration, not division.

Still, Descartes played a role in the development of mind-body dualism by developing what has become the classical argument in its favor. While there is controversy about the argument's details, its rough outlines are beyond dispute: Descartes argues that our *ideas* of mind and body are so different that, by examining them, we can establish with certainty that our minds and bodies are distinct entities:

I know that everything that I clearly and distinctly understand can be made by

God to be exactly as I understand it. That I can clearly and distinctly understand one thing apart from another is therefore enough to make me certain that it is distinct from the other, since the things can be separated by God if not by something else. (I judge the things to be distinct regardless of the power needed to make them exist separately.) Accordingly, from the fact that I have gained knowledge of my existence without noticing anything about my nature or essence except that I am a thinking thing, I can rightly conclude that my essence consists solely in the fact that I am a thinking thing. It's possible (or, as I will say later, certain) that I have a body that is very tightly bound to me. But, on the one hand, I have a clear and distinct idea of myself insofar as I am just a thinking, not an extended, thing and, on the other hand, I have a distinct idea of my body insofar as it is just an extended, not a thinking, thing. So, it's certain that I am really distinct from my body and can exist without it. (*Med. VI*, AT 7:78)

Descartes offers what he takes to be the same argument in other places—for example, in *Replies II*, when he outlines the arguments of the *Meditations* (AT 7:169–70). And he sketches another argument to the same conclusion in *Meditation VI* (AT 7:85–86). For the most part, however, my aim in this chapter will be to explicate the argument in the passage that I have just quoted—reasoning that I will call "Descartes' primary argument for dualism."

Since it will be convenient to abbreviate recurring phases, I will use "*M*" as short for "the thing that thinks Descartes' thoughts" and "*B*" as short for "the thing that is Descartes' body." Also, I will use "the *M* idea" to abbreviate "Descartes' clear and distinct idea of himself (as a thinking thing)" and "the *B* idea" to abbreviate "Descartes' clear and distinct idea of his body (as an extended thing)." In the passages quoted from *Meditation VI*, Descartes takes it for granted that both *M* and *B* exist (even though the argument for *M*'s existence does not appear until later in *Meditation VI*). He also takes it for granted that he has both the *M* idea and the *B* idea and that, since thinking and extension are different properties, the *M* idea and the *B* idea are different.

What exactly is it about the way the *M* idea differs from the *B* idea that rules out the possibility of there being a single thing in the world—a spatially extended entity with mentality—that Descartes conceives of in one way when he develops the *M* idea and in another way when he develops the *B* idea? The answer to this question will lead back to the creation of doubt in *Meditation* and the development of the Demon's Advocate in *Meditation II.*

Essence in the Argument for Dualism

Descartes thinks that, by means of his thought experiment about the piece of wax, he has developed a clear and distinct idea of a piece of wax as simply an extended thing (Chapter 7). This idea, he says, is the clear and distinct idea of any physical object—even one that we may initially conceive of as having cognitive powers such as sensing, willing, or thinking. Since we can conceive of any physical object's existing without such powers, we must regard the powers as properties of the object and delete them in the process of making our idea of that object clear and distinct.

On the other hand, according to Descartes, his clear and distinct idea of *M* (the thing that thinks his thoughts) is the idea of a thinking thing. The raw material for this idea is his prephilosophical idea of himself—the idea of a human body that moves itself, senses, and thinks (*Med. II,* AT 7:25–26). Beginning from this confused idea, he deletes everything that relates to spatial extension, leaving just the idea of a thing with the attribute of thought.[2] Thus, by the end of *Meditation II,* he takes himself to have developed both the *M* idea (his clear and distinct idea of the thing that thinks his thoughts) and the *B* idea (his clear and distinct idea of his body).

After arguing that there is a veracious God and hence that his clear and distinct ideas reliably reveal the natures of things, Descartes moves in *Meditation VI* from claims about the *M* idea and the *B* idea to conclusions about the essences of *M* and *B:* "From the fact that I have gained knowledge of my existence without noticing anything about my nature or essence except that I am a thinking thing," he writes, "I can rightly conclude that my essence consists solely in the fact that I am a thinking thing" (AT 7:78). Similarly, believing that his clear and distinct idea of *B* is simply the idea of an extended thing, he concludes that extension must be the whole essence *B.*

While we might have two different ideas of one and the same thing, it doesn't seem that we can have two different ideas of one and the same attribute. And, if thinking and extension are different attributes, it may seem to follow that *M,* whose whole essence is thinking, must be distinct from *B,* whose whole essence is extension. But there are at least two reasons for denying that, in his primary argument for dualism, Descartes does argue this way:

First, in the crucial passage from *Meditation VI,* there is only one claim about essence, "My essence consists solely in the fact that I am a thinking thing." And, after making this claim, he returns to the discussion of his ideas of *M* and *B* before stating the conclusion that *M* and *B* are distinct—something that we would not expect him to do if the sole premise from which he infers that *M* and *B* are distinct is that *M* and *B* have different essences.

Second, Descartes' contention that he can conceive of *M* apart from *B* seems to hold a prominent place in his statement of his primary argument for dualism, both in *Meditation VI* and in *Replies II.* But Descartes' demonstration that *M* and *B* have different essences rests on his examination of his clear and distinct ideas of *M* and *B, not* on the contention that *M* and *B* can exist apart from one another. Accordingly, this claim would be irrelevant to his argument if its reasoning moved directly from the claim that *M* and *B* differ in essence to the conclusion that *M* and *B* are distinct.

Third, at the end of *Replies II*—where Descartes' aim is to summarize the arguments of the *Meditations*—he does not mention essences (or natures or principle properties) even once when presenting his argument for dualism: "We clearly conceive of the mind (that is, thinking substance) apart from body (that is, substance that is extended), and conversely of body apart from mind, as everyone will readily admit. Therefore, . . . mind *can* exist without body and body without mind" (AT 7:169–70). Just a few pages before presenting this summary, he formally defined *essence* and used the notion of essence in an argument to the conclusion that God exists. If essence were central to his argument for dualism, we would expect him at least to mention it here.

Besides these textual problems, there is a logical problem with the assumption that Descartes moves directly from "*M* and *B* have different essences" to "*M* and *B* are really distinct." Suppose that attribute *A1* is the whole essence of an entity *x* and that a different attribute, *A*2, is the whole essence of an entity *y*. While it might follow that *x* and *y* are not numerically identical, it does not immediately follow that they are really distinct, since one might be semidistinct from the other. (Descartes believes that the piece of wax he considered in *Meditation II* has the attribute of extension as the whole of its essence and that God has another attribute, unbounded perfection, as the whole of His essence, but he still believes that the piece of wax is semidistinct from God—that the wax derives its existence from God and so could not possibly exist, even for a moment, without God's concourse.) Accordingly, even granted that thinking is the whole essence of *M,* that extension is the whole essence of *B,* and that thinking and extension are different attributes, he could not immediately reach the conclusion that *M* is really distinct from *B.* He would still need to say something to rule out the view (on its face, as plausible as dualism) that *M* is semidistinct from *B* and could not possibly exist without it.

That Descartes was aware of this logical problem seems clear. In *Objections V,* Gassendi attributes to *most* philosophers the view that the thing that thinks Descartes' thoughts is a form or mode of his body—something that is semidistinct from *B* (AT 7:336). And, in *Comments on a Certain Broadside,*[3] Descartes explicitly discusses the view that the mind might be a mode of body rather than something really distinct from it, acknowledging in effect that he must somehow rule out the possibility that *M* is semidistinct from *B* to establish the conclusion that *M* can exist without *B* (AT 8:350). Obviously, Descartes was aware that, to establish that *M* is really distinct from *B,* he would need to go beyond showing that *M* and *B* have different essences by establishing that neither is semidistinct from the other.

The direct—if not the only—way for Descartes to establish this would be for him to show that *M* could exist without *B* and that *B* could exist without *M.* So rather than taking him to infer the real distinctness of *M* and *B* from claims about essence alone, we might take him to be reasoning from those claims along with another premise (which he might also have derived from his claims about his ideas)—namely, that either *M* or *B* could exist without the other. And he does in fact assert this additional premise in his primary argument for dualism: "That I can clearly and distinctly understand one thing apart from another," he writes, "is . . . enough to make me certain that it is distinct from the other, since the things can be separated" (AT 7:78). But, if he could establish that M and B can exist apart from one another, premises about the essences of M and B would be otiose. According to the definition of real distinctness (Chapter 5), if M can exist without B and B can exist without M, M and B are really distinct whether or not they have different essences.

Granted, in the passage in which Descartes presents his primary argument for dualism, he does argue that the essence of M is thinking and that the essence of B is extension, and what he says about essence is important to his demonstration that M is distinct from B. Still, it seems to me to be a mistake to take him to be arguing directly from what he says about their essences to the conclusion that M and B are distinct. As I will show, while claims about essence have an important place in Descartes' argument for dualism, they do not take center stage, at least in the *Meditations*.[4]

Conceiving of Mind without Conceiving of It as Extended

As Descartes' summary of his primary argument for dualism in *Replies II* suggests, the reasoning moves from claims about the M idea and the B idea, via the principle that whatever we can clearly and distinctly grasp can exist exactly as we grasp it, to the conclusion that M and B can exist apart from one another. But how can Descartes get from premises about his ideas to conclusions about the possibility of separate existence? In particular, how can he move from his claims about the M idea to the conclusion that M can exist in a world in which there are no bodies?

At first glance, it seems that part of Descartes' argument might be this:

9.1. I can clearly and distinctly conceive of M as a thinking thing without conceiving of it as extended.
9.2. If I can clearly and distinctly conceive of something without conceiving of it as having a certain property or attribute, it's possible for that thing to without that property or attribute.
9.3. Therefore, it's possible for M to exist without being extended.

Descartes argues for premise 9.1 in *Meditation II,* premise 9.2 seems to be a version of the principle "Whatever I clearly and distinctly apprehend can be made to exist exactly as I apprehend it," to which he explicitly appeals in his primary argument for dualism, and conclusion 9.3 follows validly from premises 9.1 and 9.2.

But there are two problems with the argument from 9.1 and 9.2 to 9.3.

First, what the argument would establish, if it established anything at all, is that *M* is not itself a body. (If it were a body, extension would be its essence, and it would be impossible for it to exist without being extended.) But, as I have argued, to reach the conclusion that *M* can exist without *B,* Descartes needs to show more than that: he needs to rule out the possibility that *M* is semidistinct from *B.*

Second, as Descartes knows, premise 9.2 is unacceptable. There is nothing to prevent our saying that children just beginning their study of mathematics have clear and distinct ideas of the number seven—even though, lacking the conception of primeness, they do not conceive of seven as prime. Does it follow that seven can exist without being prime?

Arnauld raises an objection of this sort in *Objections IV.* Having imagined a person who is certain that the angle inscribed in a semicircle is a right angle (and therefore that the triangle formed by this angle and the circle's diameter is a right triangle), he imagines that this person, being ignorant of the Pythagorean theorem, doubts that the square on the triangle's hypotenuse is equal to the sum of the squares on its legs. What happens, Arnauld asks, if this person follows a course of reasoning parallel to the one Descartes offers in *Meditation VI?*

[The person whom I have imagined] clearly and distinctly understand[s] that the triangle is a right triangle without understanding that the square on the base is equal to the squares on the sides. It therefore seems to follow [on Descartes' principles] that God, at least, could possibly create a right triangle such that the square on its base is *not* equal to the squares on the sides. . . . This person falsely believes that it does not pertain to the nature of the triangle, which he clearly and distinctly knows to be a right triangle, that the square on its base [equals the squares on its sides]. Then why can't it be that I err in thinking that nothing belongs to my nature, which I clearly and distinctly know to be that of a thinking thing, other than that I am a thinking thing? Maybe it also pertains to that nature that I am an extended thing. (*Obj. IV,* AT 7:202–3)

Granting that Descartes can clearly and distinctly conceive of M as a thinking thing without conceiving of it as extended, Arnauld here challenges the inference to the conclusion that it's possible for M to exist without being extended—for, as his example indicates, we can sometimes clearly and distinctly conceive of a thing without conceiving of it as having a certain property even though the thing could not possibly exist without that property.

Descartes accepts Arnauld's criticism of 9.2. "It's possible to have the concept of [a right triangle] that does not have in it that the square on the hypotenuse is equal to the squares on the sides," he writes in *Replies IV* (AT 7:225). Notwithstanding Descartes' unqualified assertion that everything he clearly and distinctly understands can be made by God to be exactly as he understands it (AT 7:78), he therefore seems to concede that we can clearly and distinctly conceive of an object without conceiving of all that object's necessary properties, thereby admitting that 9.2 is false.

Conceiving of Mind Apart from Body

If Descartes doesn't reason from 9.1 and 9.2 to 9.3, how does he move from his claims about the idea of M the conclusion that M can exist without bodies?

A fuller statement of Descartes' reply to Arnauld in *Replies IV* suggests an answer:

> It is indeed possible to conceive of a triangle inscribed in a semi-circle without thinking that the square on the hypotenuse is equal to the sum of the squares on the legs. But it is not possible to conceive of this triangle as lacking that property. In contrast, in the case of my mind, not only can we conceive of its existing without conceiving of it as a body, but also we can deny that it has any of what that pertains to body. (AT 7:227)

The suggestion here is that the starting point of the argument for dualism is not 9.1—"I clearly and distinctly conceive of M as a thinking thing without conceiving of it as extended"—or even the stronger claim, "I can conceive of M as an unextended thing," but a claim even stronger: "I can clearly and distinctly conceive of M as existing in a way that has no connection to body whatsoever."

That the argument does depend on this stronger claim is also suggested by a shift in Descartes' language in *Meditation VI*. Having talked in the previous *Meditations* about clear and distinct ideas of entities, he now begins to use the expressions of the form "clearly and distinctly conceive of *x* apart from *y* [*unam rem absque altera clare et distincte intelligere*]" (AT 7:78; *Replies II*, AT 7:169–70). Descartes' thought here seems to be that he can clearly and distinctly conceive of a state of affairs in which *M* exists although there are no spatially extended things.

Beginning from this thought, Descartes can reason like this:

9.4, I can clearly and distinctly conceive of *M* as existing in a state of affairs in which there are no extended things.

9.5, If I can clearly and distinctly conceive of something's existing in a certain state of affairs, it's (logically) possible for the thing to exist in that state of affairs.

9.6, Therefore, it's (logically) possible for *M* to exist in a state of affairs in which there are no extended things.

Granted that extension is the essence of a body, Descartes can easily get from 9.6 to the conclusion that *M* can exist without *B*: in a world in which there are no extended things, nothing could be *B*, since (being a body in the real world) *B* could not possibly exist without being extended. Also, premise 9.5 seems to avoid the problems of 9.2, since it does not seem to entail, for instance, that the number seven could exist without being prime. So the argument from 9.4 and 9.5 to conclusion 9.6 does not face the problems that I raised in the previous section for the argument from 9.1 and 9.2 to 9.3.

Of course, the new argument has problems of its own, the chief being that it's hard to see what warrant Descartes might have for asserting its initial premise, 9.4. Still, while Descartes concedes in reply to Arnaud that 9.2 is false, he has plausible solutions to the problems with the argument from 9.4 and 9.5 to 9.6 (which I will discuss in the next section). And his contention that he can conceive of *M* existing apart from bodies is more naturally paraphrased with 9.4 than with 9.1. Accordingly, I will take the opening move of Descartes' primary argument for dualism to be the inference of 9.6 from 9.4 and 9.5.

Parallel reasoning leads Descartes to the less controversial conclusion that *B* could exist in a world devoid of mentality. Starting from the premise that he can clearly and distinctly conceive of *B* as existing in such a state, he infers (via 9.5) that *B* can exist apart from minds.

A New Role for the Demon's Advocate

As I've mentioned, the most obvious problem with the reasoning I attributed to Descartes in the last section is that he doesn't seem to have a warrant for premise 9.4: "I can clearly and distinctly conceive of *M* as existing in a state of affairs in which there are no extended things." By subtracting everything from his initial idea of himself that he can without its ceasing to be the idea of a complete thing, he produces the *M* idea, the idea simply of a thinking thing. But, just after developing this idea in *Meditation II,* he writes, "Couldn't it be that these things [namely, a rarefied gas, or air, or fire, or vapor, or breath] really aren't distinct from the 'I' that I know to exist? I don't know, and I'm not going to argue about it now" (AT 7:27). It seems clear that when Descartes has the *M* idea here, he merely conceives of *M* without conceiving of it as extended. He does not seem to be conceiving of *M* as unextended, and he certainly does not seem to be conceiving of *M* as existing in a state of affairs in which there are no bodies. Then how can he say, as he does in reply to Arnauld, that he can "deny that [*M*] has any of what pertains to body" (AT 7:227)?

My suggestion is that Descartes' answer to this question has to do with the doubts that he created in *Meditation I* and, in particular, with the device of the Demon's Advocate (Chapter 3). The Advocate may have been largely silenced in *Meditation VI,* but, if I am right, what he said when he still had his voice plays an important role in Descartes' primary argument for dualism.

In some ways, the process through which Descartes clarifies his idea of *M* parallels that by which he clarifies his idea of bodies: in both cases, he begins with an ordinary prephilosophical conception of a thing and subtracts from it everything without which it remains the conception of a complete thing. But, in another way, his procedure for the clarification of the *M* idea differs from that for the clarification of the idea of body.

Meditation II's thought experiment about the piece of wax is not connected to the method of doubt to which Descartes commits himself in *Meditation I*. (On the contrary, in the discussion of the wax, he writes as if he knows that there are pieces of wax, temporarily setting the dream hypothesis aside.) In contrast, his clarification of his idea of himself in *Meditation II* arises directly from the Cogito, the first movement out of extreme doubt. And, in the process of this clarification, Descartes sometimes speaks in the voice of the Demon's Advocate.

As I explained in Chapter 3, Descartes and the Demon's Advocate have exactly the same sensory experiences, they agree on which propositions seem obviously true, and they agree on which arguments are valid. The only difference is that, while Descartes believes his mind to be the product of a veracious God, the Advocate believes that "there is an evil demon, supremely powerful and cunning, who works as hard as he can to deceive [him]." In particular, Descartes reasons that, since it seems to him that there are physical objects, there probably are such objects, while the Advocate reasons that, since it seems to him that there are physical objects, there must not be any. "I have convinced myself," says the Advocate in *Meditation II*, "that there is nothing in the world—no sky, no earth, . . . no bodies" (AT 7:25).[5] And he maintains this position until the final paragraphs of *Meditation VI*, where the dream hypothesis is refuted.

Consider the Advocate's position after he has accepted the reasoning of the Cogito but before he has been convinced that there is a physical world. During this period, he understands what he is saying when he asserts "I am," and he therefore must have some conception of himself. But what is that conception? "What should I think now while supposing that a supremely powerful and 'evil' deceiver completely devotes himself to deceiving me?" asks Descartes (AT 7:26). He then works out an answer:

What about the things that I have assigned to soul? Nutrition and self-movement? Since I have no body, these are merely illusions. Sensing? But I cannot sense without a body, and in sleep I've seemed to sense many things that I later realized I had not really sensed. Thinking? It comes down to this: Thought and thought alone cannot be taken away from me. . . . I am not now admitting anything unless it must be true, and I therefore am not admitting that I am anything other than a thinking thing—that is, a mind, soul, understanding, or reason (terms whose meaning I did not previously know). I know that I am a real, existing thing, but what kind of thing? As I have said, a thing that thinks. (AT 7:27)

Near the beginning of this passage, the author asserts that he has no body and that he therefore does not take in nutrition, move himself, or sense a world around him. As Descartes himself has no warrant for making any of these assertions, we must take the voice here to be that of the Demon's Advocate. At this point, if we ask the Advocate what he thinks he is, he will say that he believes himself to be a thinking thing existing in a world in which there are no bodies. Accordingly, while Descartes may never conceive of himself as a thing existing in a world without bodies, the Advocate *does*. I therefore suggest that Descartes' reason for asserting premise 9.4—"I can clearly and distinctly conceive of *M* as existing in a state of affairs in which there are no extended things"—is that he thinks he did so while playing the Demon's Advocate.

By the end of the *Meditations,* Descartes is convinced that the Advocate conceived of the world inaccurately. But to establish premise 9.4, he does not need to show that *M* does now, or ever has, existed in a world without physical objects. All he needs to show is that, between the beginning of *Meditation II* and the end of *Meditation VI,* the Advocate's conception of the world is clear and distinct. If he can show this, he can move (via premise 9.5) to the conclusion that the state of affairs of which the Advocate conceives is logically possible, and that is all his argument for dualism requires.

The attention that the Advocate has paid to the development of his conception of the world may ensure that it is clear—but is there any reason for thinking that it is distinct?

This question is difficult to answer because, by the time Descartes reaches *Meditation VI*'s argument for dualism, he has stretched the meaning of the term *distinct* far beyond its original boundaries. When he first uses that phrase in the *Meditations,* it is with reference to his idea of a piece of wax (*Med. II,* AT 7:31). Later, he uses it with reference to his idea of himself (*Med. III,* AT 7:35) and his idea of God (*Med. III,* AT 7:46). In all these cases, the ideas that he calls distinct are ideas of things. While we may ultimately reject Descartes' thought that we can diminish such ideas by the intentional deletion of parts, we do at least have some grasp on what he means by calling an idea of this sort distinct: for an idea of a thing to be distinct, it must be the case that we have deleted from that idea everything that can be deleted without the idea's ceasing to be the idea of that thing. In contrast, despite the grammar of the phrase "the distinct conception of *M* existing apart from bodies," when we conceive of *M* existing apart from bodies, we are conceiving not just of *M*, but also of the circumstances of *M*'s existence. The conception in question is not an idea of a thing per se but of a thing in relation to a state of affairs. And, as far as I can see, Descartes doesn't provide us with any explanation of how we can tell whether an idea of this sort is distinct—or even of what it means to call such an idea distinct.

While this makes a rigorous assessment of premise 9.4 impossible, we can still see the general drift of Descartes' thought and appreciate its plausibility. The technical term *distinct* aside, Descartes' contention is that the Advocate's conception of the world (between *Meditation II* and *Meditation VI*) is coherent—internally consistent. Concerning the truth of this contention, I will not hazard an opinion. But it does seem to me that, if the conception is incoherent, it's not so in quite the same way as the thought that there is a right triangle that fails to satisfy the Pythagorean theorem (to take Arnauld's example). If we are sufficiently clever and industrious, we can demonstrate, simply by examining the conception of such a triangle, that no such thing exists. It is at least plausible, however, that no similarly straightforward conceptual inquiry could—or should—convince the Demon's Advocate that his idea of himself as an unextended thing existing in a world without bodies is inaccurate. If there were, Descartes would be able to use the fact that the Advocate accepts the Cogito to convince him, without appeal to the theology of *Meditations III* through *V*, that physical objects exist. But Descartes doesn't think that he can do that, and it's far from clear that he is wrong. If the Advocate says, "I exist, but there are no physical objects," what can we say to him to show, not just that what he has said is false, but that it is incoherent?

Possibility and Conceivability

From the claim that he can conceive of *M*'s existing apart from extended things and *B*'s existing apart from thinking things, Descartes infers that *M* could exist in a world devoid of extended things and *B,* in a world devoid of thinking things. "We clearly conceive of the mind (that is, thinking substance) apart from body (that is, substance that is extended), and conversely of body apart from mind, as everyone will readily admit," he writes when summarizing his argument for dualism in *Replies II.* "Therefore, . . . mind can exist without body and body without mind" (AT 7:169–70). Beneath this reasoning lies a principle about the connection of conceivability to possibility, which I will examine in this section.

The principle that the impossible cannot be imagined without confusion is so plausible that, in idiomatic English, the word *conceivable,* which originally meant "able to be mentally grasped," has come to mean "logically possible." Many thinkers after Descartes have used this principle in their reasoning, taking it to be too obvious to require justification. But, partly because he is still engaged in the quest for perfect certainty begun in *Meditation I,* Descartes attempts to derive the principle from the theology of *Meditations IV* and *V.*

In *Meditation VI,* for instance, he contends that "everything [he] clearly and distinctly understand[s] can be made by God to be exactly as [he] understand[s] it" (AT 7:78). Similarly, in *Replies II,* he adds to his arguments for God's existence the corollary that "God can make everything we clearly conceive to be exactly as we conceive it to be" (AT 7:169). Apparently, it is from these claims about God that he attempts to deduce the principle that whatever he conceives without confusion is logically possible.

Notoriously, Descartes sometimes suggests that God is above the laws of logic and that He can therefore do even what is impossible. If so, the proposition that God is sufficiently powerful to, say, separate *M* from bodies might not entail that it's possible for *M* to exist in a world without bodies.

More important, despite the impression created by the formal apparatus of propositions and corollaries at the end of *Replies II,* Descartes does not there—or anywhere else of which I am aware—offer credible proof that God *can* make things to be exactly as we clearly and distinctly conceive them to be. His only attempt begins from the general premise that there is a God "who possesses all the perfections of which we have an idea" (*Replies II*, AT 7:169). "We have in us," the argument continues, "the idea of something with so much power . . . that it can bring about everything that I understand to be possible [*intelligit ut possibilia*]." But what exactly does the phrase "understand to be possible" mean in this context? If it means "*judge* to be possible," it's far from clear that we do have the idea of something so powerful that it can bring about whatever we "understand to be possible." Apparently, as Arnauld insists, we sometimes judge something to be possible when it is not. On the other hand, if "understand to be possible" means "*correctly* judge to be possible," Descartes' argument can plausibly reach the conclusion that we can conceive of a power so great that it can bring about whatever we understand to be possible. To move from here to the conclusion that whatever we clearly and distinctly conceive is possible, however, he must assume that, whenever we clearly and distinctly conceive of something, we correctly understand that thing to be possible—exactly what he has set out to establish.

Descartes' awareness of these problems may explain why, in both *Meditation VI* and *Replies II,* after referring to God in his statement of the principle, he immediately backs away from these references. In *Meditation VI,* he says that he judges the things he clearly and distinctly understands apart from one another to be distinct, "regardless of the power needed to make them exist separately" (AT 7:78). And, in *Replies II,* he goes out of his way to explain that he mentioned God in this context, not because divine omnipotence would be needed to bring about what we clearly conceive, but because he had not yet proven the existence of anything else sufficiently powerful to make mind and body exist as we clearly conceive of them (AT 7:70).

Descartes' real reason for connecting conceivability to possibility is, I suspect, that the connection seems intuitively obvious: what we can mentally picture without confusion is, it seems, logically possible. Having argued that he can coherently picture *M*'s existing in a world devoid of bodies and *B*'s existing in a world devoid of minds, he therefore believes himself entitled to the conclusion that *M* and *B* can possibly exist apart from one another.

The Complete Argument

Believing that he can clearly and distinctly conceive of *M*'s existing in a world devoid of extended things and of *B*'s existing in a world devoid of thinking things, Descartes infers (via a premise connecting clear and distinct conception to logical possibility) that *M* could exist in a world without extended things, and *B* in a world without thinking things. From this (together with the observation that *M* is a thinking thing and *B* an extended thing), he infers that *M* and *B* are really distinct.

From a formal point of view, the argument seems invalid. If there is, say, a yellow cube that bears the two names *"A"* and *"B,"* we might reason that *A* could exist in a world in which there are no yellow things (since we can imagine a world like this one except that all the yellow things have turned red) and that *B* could exist in a world in which there are no cubic things (since we can imagine a world just like this one except that all the cubic things have become spheres)—but it obviously would be a mistake to infer that *A* and *B* are distinct.

To forestall such an objection, Descartes mentions conclusions that he established earlier when developing the *M* idea and the *B* idea: the attribute of thinking is the essence of minds (such as *M*), and the attribute of extension is the essence of bodies (such as *B*). To say that thinking is the essence of minds is to say (i) that something is a mind just in case it has the attribute of thought, and (ii) that, if something is a mind, it must have the attribute of thought in every possible world in which it exists. Thus, according to Descartes, if a thing has the attribute of thought, it would be impossible for that thing to exist without that attribute. He therefore infers that, since *B* could possibly exist in a world devoid of mentality, it could exist in a world without *M*. Similar reasoning leads him from the claim that *M* could exist in a world without extended things to the conclusion that *M* could exist in a would without *B*.

The argument therefore moves from the observation that we can clearly and distinctly conceive of *M*'s existing in a world devoid of spatial extension and of *B*'s existing in a world devoid of mentality, via premises about the essences of mind and body, to the conclusion that *M* could exist without *B*, and *B* without *M*. And, according to Descartes, the possibility of separate existence is the criterion of real distinctness.

The Mind-Body Composite

What, according to Descartes, is the relation of his mind to his body? The standard answer, correct as far as it goes, is that he advocates "two-way causal interactionism." As he sees it, acts of mind can causally affect our bodies (as when we voluntarily move our hands), and states of our bodies can causally affect our minds (as when light's striking our retinas causes us to have certain visual sensations). On Descartes' view, it seems, the mind is to the body as a sailor is to a ship. By piloting the ship by moving its rudder, the sailor performs acts that causally affect the course of the ship—and, moving along with the ship as its passenger, the sailor is causally affected by the ship's movement.

Yet, in *Meditation VI*, Descartes writes,

Through sensations such as pain, hunger, and thirst, nature . . . teaches me that I am not present in my body in the way that a sailor is present in his ship. Rather, I am very tightly bound to my body and so "mixed up" with it that we form a single thing. If this weren't so, I—who am just a thinking thing— wouldn't feel pain when my body was injured; I would perceive the injury by pure understanding in the way that a sailor sees the leaks in his ship with his eyes. And, when my body needed food or drink, I would explicitly understand that the need existed without having the mixed [*confusus*] sensations of hunger and thirst. For the sensations of thirst, hunger, and pain are just mixed modes of thought arising from the union and "mixture" of mind and body. (AT 7:81)

We can perhaps make sense of this by looking at the way in which the sailor's perceptions of the ship lead to his judgments about his well-being. After seeing a rupture in the ship's hull, the sailor *infers* that he is in jeopardy. While there may not be any conscious reasoning, it is at least as if the sailor had reasoned, "The ship's hull is ruptured; if the ship's hull is ruptured, I am in danger; therefore, I am in danger." Accordingly, even as the sailor looks at the rupture, we may be able to prevent him from forming the belief that he is in danger by getting him to hold other beliefs. For example, if the sailor believes that the rupture is a fake rigged by a movie crew, or that the ship has a special chambered hull, or that the ship has extraordinary bailing pumps, he may see the rupture and not form the belief that he is in danger. In contrast, when the dentist's drill hits a nerve, nothing that anyone might say to me will get me to do what, in the quoted passage, Descartes calls "perceiving the injury by pure understanding." In this case, the perception of injury to my body is so closely tied to my feeling that I am being harmed that it's difficult, if not impossible, to imagine dissociating the perception from the feeling. And, feeling that I am being injured, it's difficult not to pull away from the drill (even if I know "by pure understanding" that, in the long run, the drilling will be beneficial).

A dualist might hold, therefore, that sensations such as feelings of pain, thirst, and hunger are systematically misleading. Descartes would agree—insofar as those sensations incline us toward believing that our minds *are* our bodies. But he also seems to think that such sensations teach us something true and important—namely, that as human beings (rather than mere minds) we are composites of two substances, one a thinking thing and one an extended thing. Thus, in *Comments on a Certain Broadside,* he writes, "An object that we understand to possess only extension and various modes of extension is a simple entity. So is an object that we understand to have thought and various modes of thought as its sole attribute. But something that we view as having *both* extension and thought is a composite entity—a human, who is something consisting of a soul and a body" (AT 8B:351).[6] On Descartes' view, pain and other "mixed" sensations show us that we are humans rather than mere minds, by revealing that injury to our bodies is injury to us as composite entities.

According to Descartes, God has designed the relation of mind to body in this way so that our minds will immediately act to promote the interests of the mind-body composite. So, for example, when the body lacks water, the mind experiences the unpleasant sensation of thirst, which spontaneously causes the mind to act in the interests of the human being (*Med. VI,* AT 7:82).

But, if the mind is distinct from the body, why does God care about the interests of the mind-body? Descartes' answer, I guess, is that God did not create minds and bodies and then establish causal connections as an afterthought. He created humans—not mere fictions that we have invented to explain phenomena such as pain, hunger, and thirst, but real composite entities consisting of conjoined created substances of two different essences.

Because Descartes argues that his mind is distinct from his body, Gilbert Ryle accuses him (with "deliberate abusiveness") of having advocated "the Dogma of the Ghost in the Machine."[7] But, according to Descartes, a human is not merely a mind, and a mind's relation to a body—unlike, presumably, that of Ryle's ghost to its associated machine—is not purely intellectual. The mind feels what is happening to the body and views the interests of the mind-body composite as its own interests. Accordingly, although Descartes holds that mind and body are distinct entities, he maintains that, besides *understanding* the condition of the body, the mind *experiences* embodiment.

CHAPTER 10

Empirical Knowledge

In *Meditation I,* Descartes can't completely rule out the thought that all his sensory experiences might be dreams (the dream hypothesis), but these experiences provide him with his only warrant for holding particular empirical beliefs and even for holding the general belief there are physical objects. Apparently, to rescue these beliefs from doubt, he must completely rule out the dream hypothesis, silencing the Demon's Advocate once and for all.

In his attempt to do this, Descartes constructs an argument in *Meditation VI* to the conclusion that there are physical objects. While this argument's outlines are clear, its details are puzzling or obscure, as I will show. And, even if Descartes' argument for the existence of a physical world were completely successful, something more would be needed to validate his holding particular empirical beliefs, such as that he is seated before a fire. He does not attempt this validation until the final sentences of the *Meditations,* and, when he does, the attempt flies by with very little explanation, almost as an afterthought.[1] In view of the sketchiness of this reasoning, it's hard to imagine that he took himself to have ruled out the dream hypothesis definitively or to have established the truth of particular empirical propositions with perfect certainty.

But how can Descartes, who vowed not to accept anything unless he is perfectly certain of its truth, affirm particular empirical propositions when he is not perfectly certain that they are true? The answer, I suggest, is that, as he approaches the end of *Meditations,* he steps out of the project he has set for himself, returns to ordinary life, and reverts to standards of evidence less stringent than those that he adopted as he worked through the project of the *Meditations.*

The Argument for the Existence of Physical Objects

Descartes' argument for the existence of a physical world appears in this passage from *Meditation VI:*

There is in me . . . a passive ability to sense—to receive and recognize ideas of sensible things. But I wouldn't be able to put this ability to use if there weren't, either in me or in something else, an active power to produce or make sensory ideas. Since this active power doesn't presuppose understanding, and since it often produces ideas in me without my cooperation and even against my will, it cannot exist in me. Therefore, this power must exist in a substance distinct from me. And, for reasons that I've noted, either this substance is a body (corporeal nature that contains formally the reality that the ideas contain objectively) or it is God or one of His creations that is higher than a physical object (something that contains this reality eminently). But, since God isn't a deceiver, it's completely obvious that He doesn't send these ideas to me directly or by means of a creation that contains their reality eminently rather than formally. For, since He has not given me any ability to recognize that these ideas are sent by Him or by creations other than physical objects, and since He has given me a strong inclination to believe that the ideas come from physical objects, I don't see how we could understand Him to be other than a deceiver [*non esse fallacem*] if the ideas were sent to me by anything other than physical objects. It follows that physical objects exist. (AT 7:79–80)

The starting point of this reasoning is Descartes' observation that he passively receives "ideas of sensible things." Believing that everything present in an idea must be present in something that causes that idea (Chapter 5), he infers that something containing extension must cause these ideas. To this point, the reasoning resembles his first argument for God's existence in *Meditation III*—an argument in which he moves from the observation that one of his ideas contains infinite greatness objectively to the conclusion that the idea must have a cause that contains infinite greatness formally.

But do the causes of our ideas of sensible things contain extension formally, rather than eminently (Chapter 5)? That is, do they contain extension in a way that entails that they are bodies, as opposed to the way that it is present in God, who is incorporeal? To show that answer is yes, Descartes constructs an argument reminiscent of *Meditation IV*'s validation of clear and distinct apprehension. We have a "strong inclination" to believe that the causes of our ideas of sensible things are physical objects (he says) and we can trust these inclinations since God is not a deceiver.

"Ideas of Sensible Things"

What might Descartes mean by the expression "ideas of sensible things" [*ideae rerum sensibilium*]? A plausible guess (which many have endorsed) is that the "sensible things" in question are extended created substances and therefore that the phrase "ideas of sensible things" refers to our sensations of such things—the experiences we have when it seems to us that we detect such created substances with our eyes, hands, and so on. On this guess, Descartes' assertion that he receives ideas of sensible things is equivalent to the assertion that he has certain sensory experiences (like that of sensing a table). And this reading seems confirmed by his insistence that the ideas of sensible things come to him "without his cooperation" and "against his will." Generally speaking, while we can turn our heads or close our eyes, we passively receive the visual experiences that happen to come to us when we stand still with eyes open. (When arguing in the *Principles* that physical objects exist, Descartes notes that "it is not in our power to make it the case that we sense one thing rather than another, as what we sense depends entirely on the thing that affects our senses" [AT 8:40].)

Yet, in *Meditation II*, Descartes argues at length that physical objects "are not grasped by the senses or the power of having mental images, but by understanding alone" (AT 7:34)—that what we sense, the truly sensible things, are just modes of such substances (AT 7:32). It therefore seems unlikely that in *Meditation VI* he would say that our ideas of extended created substances are the ideas of *sensible* things.[2]

A clue to the solution to this problem may appear at the beginning of Part II of the *Principles,* where Descartes offers an argument for the existence of physical objects similar in overall structure, if not in detail, to the argument I have quoted from *Meditation VI*:[3]

Surely, what we sense unquestionably comes from something distinct from our minds—for it is not in our power to make it the case that we sense one thing rather than another, as what we sense depends entirely on the thing that affects our senses. Still, we can ask whether that thing is God or something distinct from God. Since we sense or, rather, are stimulated by sense to clearly and distinctly apprehend material objects extended in length, breadth, and depth whose parts have various shapes and move in various ways producing the various sensations we have of colors, smells, pain, and so on, if God presented the idea of extended matter to us directly and by Himself or if He presented that idea to us by means of something other than Himself in which there was no extension, shape, or motion, there would not be any conceivable defense against the accusation that He is a deceiver—for we clearly understand the matter [by means of which God produces that idea in us] to be something completely distinct from Him and from us (or our minds), and we seem to see that the idea of this matter comes from something outside our minds that resembles that idea completely. But, as I've noted, it is clearly inconsistent with God's nature that He be a deceiver. Therefore, we must conclude without reservation that there is something extended in length, breadth, and depth and that has all the properties we clearly apprehend to belong to extended things. (AT 8:40–41)

At one point in this reasoning, Descartes starts to infer the existence of physical objects from the observation that we *sense* them: "Since we sense . . . material objects . . . , we must conclude without reservation that there is something extended in length, breadth, and depth." But he corrects himself. The existence of physical objects does not follow from the fact that we sense (or seem to sense), he suggests, but from the fact that we "are stimulated by sense to clearly and distinctly apprehend material objects."

The correction reminds us, if a reminder was needed, that Descartes distinguishes our sensations of the material world from our clear and distinct ideas of physical objects. On the other hand, that he allowed the correction to stand rather than simply crossing out the false start suggests that, at least in this context, he does not scrupulously insist on the distinction. In his view, we have various sensations and are "stimulated" [*impulsi*] by those sensations to develop clear and distinct ideas of physical objects. Whether we take the starting point of the argument to be the observation that we have the sensations or the fact that we have the clear and distinct ideas that we derive from those sensations seems not to make much difference to him.

Reading this thought back into the argument of *Meditation VI*, we might suspect that Descartes does not use the phrase "ideas of sensible things" simply to refer to sensations that seem to be caused by physical objects. He may also apply this phrase to our clear and distinct ideas of physical things—ideas of extended things that, though stimulated by sensation, do not present physical objects to us as things that we do, or even can, sense.

The reading may be strained, but what are the alternatives to it? "I comprehend with my judgment, which is in my mind, [physical] objects that I once believed myself to see with my eyes," Descartes writes in *Meditation II* (AT 7:32). Are we to suppose that, in *Meditation VI*, he turns around and takes these very entities to be "sensible things"?

The Origins of Our "Strong Inclinations"

Whatever exactly Descartes counts as "ideas of sensible things," he thinks that, when we consider these ideas, we are strongly inclined toward believing that they come from spatially extended entities. But why think that this inclination rests on something less dubious than what Descartes himself calls "childhood prejudices" (AT 8:40)? In both *Meditation VI* and the *Principles,* he insists that we are passive in the reception of certain ideas, but this shows only that we do not produce those ideas in ourselves. In his view, what is it about our ideas of the world that "inclines" us toward thinking that some of them come from physical objects?

Descartes' distinction of three stages of sensation in *Replies VI* (AT 7:436–38) may point toward an answer. The first stage of sensation, he says, is simply the effect of an object external on one of our organs of sense—an effect that he believes "must consist entirely in the motion of the particles in those organs." The second stage, he says, "includes all the immediate effects that are produced in the mind because it is united with the affected bodily organ—such as the perceptions of pain, pleasure, thirst, hunger, color, sound, taste, smell, heat, cold, and so on." The third stage, he says, "includes all the judgments about objects outside us occasioned by the motions of our bodily organs that we have been accustomed to make from infancy." To illustrate the judgments associated with the third stage, he supposes that—as a result of his experiencing certain sensations of color—he infers that there is a stick at a certain distance from him that has a certain size and shape.

Descartes admits that, since "the third stage of sensation" involves rational calculation and "depends solely on the intellect" (AT 7:438), it is not, strictly speaking, a stage of sensation at all. We only regard it as sensory, he explains, because we make the inferences habitually and without reflection (AT 7:438).

While Descartes may not think that we achieve the third stage of sensation from birth, he does repeatedly say that we do so from our earliest years [*ab ineunte aetate*]. He does not seem to think that others teach us to make the inferences associated with this stage, or even that we learn how to make them though experience. Apparently, he views the inferences as natural in that, as a consequence of the designs of our minds, we spontaneously draw them when we experience certain sensations.

According to Descartes, however, there are at least two reasons for thinking that we can prevent ourselves from drawing such inferences and hence that, until we complete the argument of *Meditation VI*, our Wills are not *compelled* to affirm the proposition "Physical objects exist."

First, if our Wills were compelled to affirm that proposition, it would be impossible for us to suppose or feign that there are no physical objects. Even the Demon's Advocate can never bring himself to assert flatly that two plus three is other than five; the best he can do is to say that every proposition in a certain class is false and that "2 + 3 = 5" is in that class (Chapter 3). But the Advocate does flatly assert that there are no physical objects. "I have convinced myself that there is nothing in the world," he says in *Meditation I*, "no sky, no earth, no minds, no bodies."

Second, when arguing for the existence of physical objects in *Meditation VI,* Descartes considers (and rules out) the hypotheses that he is the cause of his ideas of such objects, that God is their cause, and that nonphysical creations of God are their cause—and he claims that, if these ideas were caused by anything other than physical objects, there would be no way for him to discover that fact. If he thought that we were compelled to believe that physical objects exist, none of this would have been necessary. He could simply have pointed back to *Meditation IV,* where he "proved" that whatever his Understanding compels his Will to believe is true.

Still, since Descartes thinks that it's natural (in the way I have explained) to draw inferences about existing objects in "the third stage of sensation," and since he thinks that we draw these inferences without even noticing that we are doing so, it seems safe to assume that, in his view, it would be extremely difficult to prevent ourselves from drawing them. This seems to accord with experience: when we have certain sensations, we are strongly, though not irresistibly, moved toward judging that there are physical objects before us.

These inclinations can be called sensory in that they are occasioned by sensations (which we receive in the second stage of sensation). But the inclinations themselves are dispositions to move from the presence of certain sensations to the judgment that there are physical objects of certain sorts—a judgment formed by the Understanding and affirmed by the Will. And the world whose existence Descartes seeks to establish on the basis of these inclinations is not a world of colors, tastes, odors, and other such sensible qualities, but a world of objects presented to us by our (nonsensory) clear and distinct idea of physical objects as extended things—objects whose "nature is the subject-matter of pure mathematics" (AT 7:74).

What We Couldn't Know

When arguing for the existence of physical objects, Descartes contends that, if the causes of our sensory ideas were not extended, there would be no way for us to discover that fact. As far as I can see, he makes no attempt to explain or support this contention. But we may be able to supply the missing explanation if we imagine someone who tries to prove that our ideas of physical objects come from things that are not (formally) extended. There does not seem to be any way for this person to construct his proof a priori; while the examination of our clear and distinct idea of physical objects may show that its cause must contain extension, nothing in it reveals—or, apparently, *could* reveal—that its cause contained extension eminently (rather than formally). Appeals to natural inclinations don't seem to help either, since all our inclinations are toward believing that our ideas of physical objects do come from physical objects. The only other way to show that the causes of our ideas of physical objects are not formally extended, it seems, would require appeal to empirical evidence. But here again the attempt seems hopeless; whatever we notice about our ideas will be consistent with the view that the causes of our ideas of physical objects are things that contain extension formally, not just eminently.

"God Does Not Deceive"

From the proposition that there is a veracious God, Descartes infers that, if we are strongly inclined to believe a proposition and nothing that we might discover would reveal to us that the proposition is false, that proposition must be true. Obviously, there is a parallel here to his view that a veracious God would not have so misdesigned his mind that his Will was compelled to affirm a proposition when that proposition was in fact false (Chapter 6). But, if what I suggested above is right, there is an important difference between being compelled to believe and merely being strongly inclined to believe. If we are just strongly inclined, we can (in theory) successfully resist. And, in *Meditation IV,* Descartes argued that we always go wrong by affirming propositions that we can prevent ourselves from affirming—even if they happen to be true (AT 7:59–60). Then why should the fact that we are strongly inclined to affirm that there are physical objects lead us to believe that there are such objects?

In the *Meditations* (unlike the *Principles*), Descartes' answer seems to have to do with the limitations of our ability to correct errors. As he sees it, we can be sure that whatever we are compelled to believe is true, since "there is no faculty as reliable as the light of nature by means of which [we] could learn that [such things are] not true" (AT 7:38–39). In contrast, there does not seem to be any way generally to rule out the possibility that we might sometimes be strongly inclined (rather than compelled) to believe propositions that we later discover to be false.[4] But Descartes' view is that, in the case of the proposition "Physical objects exist," there is no such possibility. As he sees it, God has not given him "any ability to recognize that [his ideas of sensory things] have been sent by [God himself] or by creations other than physical objects" (AT 7:79–80). So God would be deceptive unless these ideas were in fact caused in him by a physical world.

The reasoning here seems to be moral: When we believe that a proposition is true when in fact it is false, we err. If we could somehow have discovered that the proposition was false, responsibility for the error would be ours; God can't be blamed for what happens due to our lack of diligence. On the other hand, if we were strongly inclined to affirm a proposition by virtue of our God-given natures and there were no way for us to discover that the proposition was false, responsibility for the error we would commit by affirming that proposition would be God's. Therefore, if we have yielded to a strong God-given inclination to affirm a false proposition when there is no way for us to discover that the proposition is false (Descartes seems to argue), God—a perfectly moral being—would be blameworthy.

But this reasoning doesn't reach the desired conclusion. At best, what it shows is that, if Descartes *had* yielded to his strong, God-given inclination to affirm that there are physical objects and nothing that he might discover would show him that there are no such objects, that proposition would have to be true. But, as he begins his proof for the existence of the physical world, he *hasn't* yielded to this inclination. Having accepted the dream hypothesis, the Demon's Advocate denies the existence of physical objects in *Meditation I,* and nothing between *Meditation I* and *Meditation VI* has caused him to change his mind on this point. But Descartes has resolved not to affirm any proposition unless he can convince the Advocate of its truth. So, as Descartes begins *Meditation VI,* he suspends judgment on the question of whether there are physical objects. If there were no physical objects, God would not be responsible for Descartes' error of thinking that there are, because Descartes hasn't committed that error.

For comparison, consider the following story: Although he was born in New York, an acquaintance tells me that he was born in Ohio—adding immediately that, since he is in a playful mood, it wouldn't be prudent for me to believe everything that he has said about himself. Because of his warning, I prevent myself from believing that he was born in Ohio. I am (let's suppose) inclined toward that belief; if I were forced to bet one way or the other, I would choose to bet that he was born there. But, when not under pressure, I sincerely say that I don't know where this person was born.

Since my acquaintance's saying that he was born in Ohio would ordinarily lead me to believe that he was born there, he would initially have set up an inclination toward affirming a false proposition. Still, few would say that he had deceived. As we ordinarily use the term *deceive*, to deceive people is to induce them to hold false beliefs. And, in this case, because of his warning, I didn't come to hold such a belief.

But Descartes seems committed to saying that, if there were no physical objects, his relation to the proposition "Physical objects exist" would be similar to my relation to the proposition that my friend was born in Ohio. Distinguishing propositions that our God-given natures compel us to affirm from those they strongly incline us to affirm, he reasons that, while we never go wrong by affirming propositions of the first sort, we always go wrong by affirming propositions of the second sort. It therefore seems that, by designing Descartes' mind in a way that allowed him to see this, God has given him the ability to see that he would err by affirming the proposition "Physical objects exist" and therefore the ability to see that he ought to withhold his assent from that proposition. But, if Descartes does not affirm that physical objects exist, what point is there to saying that God would be deceiving him unless they do exist?[5]

What I have presented as a criticism of Descartes' argument may, however, simply point to a shortcoming of translation. Like others,[6] I have translated clauses of the form *Deus non est fallax* with "God is not a deceiver." An equally faithful but more charitable interpretation might be "God is not deceptive," or even "God does not mislead."[7] If we accept such a translation, we sidestep the objection I have raised—for, to be deceptive, it's not necessary to succeed in deceiving. If there were no physical objects (Descartes might say), the arrangement of God's creation would be misleading simply because our natures would naturally lead us to view the world is a certain way when in fact it was not that way.

But, if the retranslation solves one problem, it raises another. The view that God is not a deceiver seems to follow from Descartes' contention that God is morally perfect when conjoined to our ordinary moral judgments concerning deceivers. But, if God can be deceptive without actually deceiving anyone, why think that a perfectly moral God *can't* be deceptive? In the case of the deceptive acquaintance, it's far from clear that he was immoral, since he himself prevented me from forming false beliefs about where he was born. And, if the misleading friend isn't immoral, why suppose that a misleading God would be?

Descartes may indicate the solution to this problem in *Meditation IV*, when he suggests that a benevolent being would be deceptive only if he were weak (AT 7:53). The thought, it seems, is that—being omnipotent and omniscient—a benevolent God would create the world straightforwardly, with no unnecessary complications. But what would be the necessity of God's endowing us with the strong inclination to believe that there are physical objects if there were none? God could (it seems) have designed our minds so that we did not move from the second to the third stage of sensation. And, if there were no physical objects, wouldn't the world be less complex if he had done so?

My suggestion, then, is that *Meditation VI*'s argument for the existence of physical objects does not rest squarely on moral intuitions, but at least in part on intuitions about elegance. Descartes might plausibly argue that, if there were no physical objects, something would be wrong even if we don't acquire false beliefs about their existence: the world that God created would display bad craftsmanship in that some of the things in it—namely our minds—would spontaneously draw false inferences. And, quite apart from considerations of the morality of deception, an omnipotent and omniscient God would not have built such complexity into his creation unless things were somehow better with it than without it.

The Dream Hypothesis Revisited

Once Descartes completes the argument for the existence of the physical world, he views himself as having ruled out the most extreme version of the dream hypothesis—the thought that he is a disembodied mind living in a completely immaterial universe. Still, immediately after completing this argument, he goes on to write, "What about particular properties, such as the size and shape of the sun? And what about things that I understand less clearly than mathematical properties, like light, sound, and pain? These are [still] open to doubt" (AT 7:80). And he is right, of course. Granting that physical objects cause our ideas of sensible things and therefore that the world of matter exists, we can still suspect that our ideas do not accurately reveal to us anything about that world other than that it exists (and, perhaps, that we can describe it in the language of mathematics and geometry). That is, while Descartes' argument for the existence of matter may rule out the hypothesis that he is a disembodied mind living in an immaterial universe, it does not by itself rule out more limited versions of the dream hypothesis—such as that he was dreaming on every occasion on which he seemed to acquire sensory evidence that the sun is spherical.

That may be why, after arguing for the existence of physical objects in the middle of *Meditation VI,* Descartes redirects his attention to the dream hypothesis in the *Meditations'* final paragraph:

I know that sensory indications of what is good for my body are more often true than false, I can almost always examine a given thing with several senses, and I can also use my memory (which connects the present to the past) and my understanding (which has now examined all the causes of error). Hence, I need no longer fear that what the senses daily show me is unreal. I should reject the exaggerated doubts of the past few days as ridiculous. This is especially true of the chief ground for these doubts—namely, my inability to distinguish dreaming from being awake. For I now notice that dreaming and being awake are importantly different: the events in dreams are not linked by memory to the rest of my life like those that happen while I am awake. . . . If I distinctly observe something's source, its place, and the time at which I learn about it, and if I grasp an unbroken connection between it and the rest of my life, I'm quite sure that it is something in my waking life rather than in a dream. And I ought not to have the slightest doubt about the reality of such things if I have examined them with all my senses, my memory, and my understanding without finding any conflicting evidence. For, from the fact that God is not a deceiver, it follows that I am not deceived in any case of this sort. (AT 7:89–90)

In effect, Descartes here contends that he can refute limited versions of the dream hypotheses in roughly the same way as he refuted the extreme version. Suppose, for example, that when he looks at a ball, it seems to him to be spherical. There are only three ways (he suggests) that he might find out that these appearances are misleading: he might examine the ball with senses other than sight, he might compare his present experiences of the ball to past experiences, or he might reason about the ball—using sense, memory, and reason. If none of these challenges the view that the ball is spherical, it follows that the ball is spherical—because (as established in the general proof of the existence of physical objects) God, who does not mislead, would not have given him the strong inclination to believe a false proposition unless he also gave him the ability to discover that the proposition was false. Thus, according to Descartes, while his present sensory experiences do not by themselves warrant perfect certainty that there is a spherical ball before him, they do warrant certainty on these matters when conjoined to the observation that a complete examination of the situation would not yield any evidence against the claim that there is a spherical ball before him.

While Descartes made a point of saying in *Meditation I* "that there are no reliable signs by which [he] can distinguish sleeping from waking" (AT 7:19), he now claims to have discovered such a sign: if there is an unbroken connection between a given experience and the rest of our lives (he says), that experience must be from our waking lives, not a dream.

But an appeal to this principle could justify our being perfectly certain of the truth of a particular empirical proposition only if we were perfectly certain that there was an unbroken connection between given experiences and the rest of our lives. And how could we ever be perfectly certain of that? For each of us, part of our life is in the future, unknown. If we don't now know what the whole of our lives will be like, how can we say with perfect certainty of any experience that it is connected in the way that Descartes requires? A similar point can be made about the past: when we check to see whether a present experience coheres with the rest of our lives, how can we ever be perfectly certain that we have recalled every relevant experience?

Take, for example, my present experience of the desk before me. Suppose that I "observe its source, its place, and the time at which I learned about it, and that I grasp with memory an unbroken connection between it and the rest of my life"—or, rather, my life *so far*. And suppose that, having done all this, I raise the question of whether my present experience of the desk is part of a dream. I see no way to establish with *perfect* certainty that, in the next moment, the desk won't seem to me inexplicably to disappear. And, if that were to happen, I might conclude, on Cartesian principles, that the desk was an illusion. But, if I must now—at time *t*—concede the possibility that future experiences might justify my withdrawing the judgment that the desk exists at *t*, I can't claim to be perfectly certain at *t* that the desk does exist. As I argued in Chapter 2, perfect certainty implies perfect stability.

And what are we to make of Descartes' assertion that "events in dreams are not linked by memory to the rest of [his] life like those that happen while [he is] awake"? How exactly *are* the events in our waking lives linked to one another? Complete coherence is too much to require. (Although I clearly recall putting my keys down on the table as I came into my office, they're not there now—but I still think that I am awake.) Even radical discontinuity is not always taken as a sign that our experiences are illusory. (If a boxer who is knocked out in the ring awakens in a hospital, he may not infer that he is dreaming even though his last memory is of a place very different from the one in which he now finds himself.) So, while we might grant that our experiences in dreams don't relate to our life stories in the same way as our veridical experiences, the precise nature of the difference would be hard to spell out. But, until we have a clear and explicit understanding of that difference, there will always be some uncertainty as to whether a given experience is part of a dream.

The Program's End

Descartes' aim in trying to refute the dream hypothesis is to show that, in theory, we can know some empirical propositions to be true with perfect certainty. Immediately after rejecting this hypothesis as ridiculous, however, he hints (in the *Meditations'* final sentence) that he will not always strive for such certainty in practice. "Since the need to act does not always allow time for such a careful examination," he writes, "we must admit the likelihood of men's erring about particular things and acknowledge the weakness of our nature" (AT 7:91).

If we require that we be perfectly certain of a proposition's truth before we affirm it, our system of beliefs will be stable—but very small. Life is short, the attainment of perfect certainty takes time, and (regardless of how diligent or clever we are) we may not be able to attain perfect certainty with respect to all propositions that are important to us. On the other hand, if we allow ourselves to affirm propositions of whose truth we are not perfectly certain, our system of beliefs will be larger and better able to inform our actions—but less stable and more likely to contain errors. Assuming that Descartes does not expect us to ignore our need to act, we can take the final sentence of the *Meditations* to suggest a compromise: while we should of course be as careful in the acquisition of beliefs as time allows (he seems to say), we should sometimes accept beliefs about which we have some doubt when failure to do so would leave us without proper guides to action.

The position seems reasonable. Suppose that, when a woman who is standing at the bottom of a hill looks up and sees a large boulder rolling down toward her, she is inclined to believe that she can save herself by stepping aside. According to Descartes, it would be *possible* (in some sense of that term) for her to examine her belief using sense, memory, and reason and so to achieve certainty that the belief is true. But, since the boulder might hit her in the first few moments of such an examination, she apparently should allow herself to hold the belief even though she has some slight doubts about it. Perfect certainty may be desirable, but it is not the only thing that can reasonably be desired.

Yet, in *Meditation IV,* Descartes seemed to have insisted that we strive for perfect certainty without compromise:

When I limit my will's range of judgment to the things presented clearly and distinctly to my understanding, I obviously cannot err. . . . Today, then, I have learned what to avoid in order not to err and also what to do to reach the truth. I surely will reach the truth if I just attend to the things that I understand perfectly and distinguish them from those that I grasp more obscurely and confusedly. And that is what I'll take care to do from now on. (AT 7:62)

How can Descartes make this resolution in *Meditation IV* and then go on in *Meditation VI* to suggest that we should affirm some propositions of which we are not perfectly certain?

The answer, it seems, is that, in the final sentence of *Meditation VI,* he is ending the *Meditations'* project. The project had a definite aim to be achieved by application of a definite method. The aim was the development of a system of perfectly certain beliefs, and the method was adherence to a rule that began as "Affirm a proposition only if you can convince the Demon's Advocate of its truth" and later became "Affirm only those propositions that you clearly and distinctly apprehend." There was never any thought that this project would go on forever. On the contrary, at the beginning of the *Meditations,* Descartes says that he will attempt this project "once in his life," and he indicates that he has arranged—temporarily, one might suppose—for the seclusion that the project will require (AT 7:17–18). Eventually, he will leave the meditative life and return to an ordinary life of action. But, as he himself says in his *Discourse on Method* (1637), "in practical life it is sometimes necessary to act on opinions that one knows to be uncertain just as though they were indubitable" (AT 6:31).

But, if Descartes allows himself to have uncertain beliefs after he has completed the project of the *Meditations,* what was the point of his scrupulously avoiding such beliefs during the project? What difference does it make whether uncertainty creeps in at the beginning of the project or floods in at its end?

The answer may lay in the architectural metaphor that Descartes introduces in the first sentence of *Meditation I.* Our system of beliefs, he implies, is like a building—with foundations and a structure built on those foundations. Descartes' concern in the *Meditations* is largely with the foundations. His worry is not that people may disagree about the truth of particular empirical propositions but that they might disagree about the basic principles of "first philosophy"—such as that our minds are reliable instruments for the detection of truth or that material objects exist or that God exists. Once he takes himself to have established these principles with perfect certainty, he is prepared to compromise—just as a builder who has laid very stable foundations might relax his standards when installing outside trim. The whole building will fall if the foundations crumble, but nothing of much moment will result from damage to other parts of the structure.

That may explain why, having presented the dream hypothesis in *Meditation I* with great fanfare, Descartes does such a sketchy job of refuting it in *Meditation VI*. While he does want to establish the theoretical possibility of our knowing particular empirical propositions with perfect certainty, he recognizes that the demands of practical life will often, if not always, require our settling for much less.

Notes

1. Descartes' *Meditations on First Philosophy* (*Meditations de Prima Philoso-phiae*) was published, in Latin, in 1641. References to the *Meditations* and to Descartes' other writings are by volume and page to Descartes, *Oeuvres de Des-cartes,* ed. Charles Adam and Paul Tannery (Paris: Leopold Cerf, 1904). While the translations are generally my own, I will sometimes refer to the English translation in *The Philosophical Writings of Descartes,* trans. John Cottingham, Robert Stoothoff, and Dugald Murdoch (Cambridge: Cambridge University Press, 1984), whose margins indicate the corresponding "AT" numbers.

2. Originally published with *Meditations,* the writings called *Objections and Replies* include critical comments on the *Meditations* by several of Descartes' contemporaries along with his replies. The second set of objections, which was published anonymously, may have been the work of Marin Mersenne.

CHAPTER I

1. That we doubt that p at time t does not of course entail that we are con-sidering "p" at that time. Even when in dreamless sleep, we can doubt that there is a largest prime number.

2. George Berkeley, *Three Dialogues between Hylas and Philonous,* ed. David Hilbert and John Perry (Claremont, Calif.: Areté Press, 1994), 8.

3. This definition is suggested by Edwin M. Curley's analysis of "valid grounds for doubt." See his *Descartes against the Skeptics* (Oxford: Blackwell, 1978), esp. 122. For my differences with Curley, see my review of this work in *British Journal for the Philosophy of Science* 31 (1980): 104–8.

4. There is a technical difficulty here, which I will ignore in what follows. On the one hand, it seems too much to ask that the hypothesis entail that not-p by itself; as the case of the juror suggests, adopting this strict criterion for the application of the phrase "directly challenges" would force us to say that some

rival theories of the crime do not directly challenge the juror's belief. On the other hand, it seems too little to ask that the hypothesis entails that not-*p* when conjoined to all *A*'s beliefs; adopting this liberal criterion for the application of the phrase "directly challenges" would force us to say that, if *A* believes that not-*p* (or his system of beliefs is inconsistent in any other way), any hypothesis whatever would directly challenge his belief that *p*.

5. Among the Pyrrhonian works known to Descartes were Sextus Empiricus' *Outline of Pyrrhonianism* and Michel Montaigne's *In Defense of Raymond Sabond*. See Richard H. Popkin, *The History of Scepticism from Erasmus to Spinoza* (Berkeley: University of California Press, 1979).

6. Another possible objection to the identification of belief with affirmation of the Will is that, while there are degrees of belief, one's Will either assents to a proposition fully or not at all. But, for any person *A* and any proposition "*p*," isn't it either completely true or completely false that *A* believes that *p*? When people talk about degrees of belief, I suggest, they are really talking, in a somewhat misleading way, about degrees of certainty.

7. Locke takes up the question of how arguments persuade in the fourth book of his *Essay*. See John Locke, *An Essay Concerning Human Understanding*, ed. A. C. Fraser (New York: Dover, 1959). More recent philosophers have tended to shuttle the question off to psychologists, who seem disposed to hand it back.

CHAPTER 2

1. Bernard Williams, *Descartes: The Project of Pure Enquiry* (Sussex: Harvester Press, 1978), 48.

2. Janet Broughton, *Descartes's Method of Doubt* (Princeton, N.J.: Princeton University Press, 2003), 51.

3. See Thomas Kuhn, *The Copernican Revolution: Planetary Astronomy in the Development of Western Thought* (Cambridge, Mass.: Harvard University Press, 1957).

CHAPTER 3

1. *Objections VII,* which first appeared in the second edition of the *Meditations* (1642), was written by Pierre Bourdin, a Jesuit.

2. Harry G. Frankfurt, *Demons, Dreamers, and Madmen: The Defense of Reason in Descartes' Meditations* (New York: Bobbs-Merrill, 1970), 17.

3. The word *trope,* which is used in this way by skeptics including Sextus Empiricus, derives from the Greek word for "turn," and Descartes says that he is going to use the method to "turn his Will around" [*in contrarium versa*] (*Med. I,* AT 7:22).

4. See Sextus Empiricus, "Outlines of Pyrrhonism," part 1, chap. 14, in *Sextus Empiricus: Selections from the Major Writings on Scepticism, Man, and God,* ed. Philip P. Hallie (Indianapolis: Hackett, 1985), 44–72.

5. Descartes seems to have written the *Rules* [*Regulae ad Directionem Ingenii*], which were published posthumously, before 1628, more than a dozen years before the publication of the *Meditations.*

6. On this point, I am in agreement with Frankfurt, who writes, "Unless Descartes supposes himself to be sane he cannot conduct the investigation to which he wishes to devote himself" (*Demons,* 38).

7. In *Descartes's Method of Doubt* (Princeton, N.J.: Princeton University Press, 2003), Janet Broughton considers what she calls "the lunacy argument," contending that Descartes produces grounds for doubt in *Meditation I* by considering the hypothesis that he might be a madman. (See, for example, 21–22 and 62–64.) In fact, the only mention of madmen in *Meditation I* comes in the passage about paupers who think they are kings (AT 7:19), which ends with the sentence, "But these people are insane, and I would seem just as crazy if I were to apply what I say about them to myself." Descartes' aim here, as I understand it, is not to raise the hypothesis that he might be a lunatic, but to dismiss that hypothesis out of hand. As the *Meditations* go on and he attempts to settle the doubts of *Meditation I,* he frequently returns to the dream hypothesis and the hypothesis of the evil demon, but he never again mentions madmen or lunatics—not at the end of *Meditation I,* where he resolves to treat the dream hypothesis and the hypothesis of the evil demon as true, or in *Meditation IV,* where he settles doubts about nonempirical propositions, or in *Meditation VI,* where he settles doubts about empirical propositions.

8. This concern with method is evident in the titles of several of Descartes' works, such as *Discourse on Method* and *Rules for the Direction of the Mind.*

CHAPTER 4

1. The slogan "*cogito ergo sum*" does not appear in the *Meditations* itself, but Descartes uses similar wording—"*ego cogito, ergo sum, sive existo,*" meaning "I think, therefore I am or exist"—in *Replies II* (AT 7:140).

2. Jaaco Hintikka, "Cogito, Ergo Sum: Inference or Performance," in *Descartes: A Collection of Critical Essays,* ed. Willis Doney (Notre Dame: University of Notre Dame Press, 1968), 108–39. This article originally appeared in *Philosophical Review* 71 (1962).

3. Hintikka, "Cogito, Ergo Sum," 122.

4. Janet Broughton, *Descartes's Method of Doubt* (Princeton, N.J.: Princeton University Press, 2003), 99. For consistency of style, I have substituted "*p*" for Broughton's expression "(*B*)."

5. Broughton sketches two lines of reasoning that Descartes might use in the attempt to prove premise 4.4 to the Demon's Advocate, one based on the general observation that doubting happened in *Meditation I* and another based on consideration of the particular hypothesis whose consideration led to that doubting (117–19). But this simply pushes the problem back one step: presented with these arguments, the Advocate would reject their premises for exactly the same reason that he rejects every other proposition that seems obviously true to him.

6. Inasmuch as he here has the confused idea of himself as a body permeated by soul (AT 7:26), the dream hypothesis may also provide him with what seem to him to be valid grounds for doubting his own existence.

7. Hintikka, "Cogito, Ergo Sum," 114.

CHAPTER 5

1. See Francisco Suarez, *Disputationes Metaphysicae I* (Hildensheim: Georg Olms, 1965), disputation 7, 250–74.

2. Descartes published *The Principles of Philosophy* in 1644, three years after the *Meditations,* intending that it be used as a textbook. References to the *Principles* are to vol. 8A of Descartes, *Oeuvres de Descartes,* ed. Charles Adam and Paul Tannery (Paris: Leopold Cerf, 1904).

3. Of course, on definition 5.2, *A* and *B* might be really distinct without our being willing to count them as two. While a car might exist without its carburetor and the carburetor without the car, they are not two distinct things, since one is a part of another.

4. Taking the real distinction to hold only between (created) substances, Descartes acknowledges a second form of the modal distinction: "the distinction between two modes of the same substance" (AT 8:29). In what follows, I will ignore this second form.

5. John Locke, *An Essay Concerning Human Understanding,* ed. A. C. Fraser (New York: Dover, 1959), book 2, chap. 8.

6. I will discuss Descartes' doctrine of eminent presence later.

7. Anthony Kenny, *Descartes: A Study of His Philosophy* (New York: Random House, 1968), 134.

8. R. S. Woolhouse, *Descartes, Spinoza, Leibniz: The Concept of Substance in Seventeenth Century Metaphysics* (New York: Routledge, 1993), 17.

9. In his *Ethics,* Spinoza argues that God is the only substance and therefore that everything else that exists must be a mode of substance. See, for example, the proof of part 1, prop. 15. Baruch Spinoza, *Ethics,* trans. Samuel Shirley (Indianapolis: Hackett, 1991), 40.

10. Understandably, some translate Descartes' verb *representire* (for example, at AT 7:40, line 11) with the English "represent," making it seem that, accord-

ing to Descartes, an idea represents its object. A better translation, however, is "present." On Descartes view, the idea of *x* presents *x* to us as an object of our thought.

11. "Everything that is called imperfect is held to be imperfect because of a diminution of what is perfect," writes Boethius in *The Consolation of Philosophy* (book 3, chap. 10). "So, if we find that something of a certain kind is imperfect, there must also be something else of that same kind that it perfect. For, if we ignore the perfect, we cannot even imagine the origin of the existence of that which we hold to be imperfect." Boethius, *Philosophiae Consolationis,* ed. Karl Buchner (Heidelberg: Winter, 1977), 57. (The translation is mine.)

12. See, for example, Locke, *Essay,* book 2, chap. 17, § 1–3.

13. The Latin phrase that I here translate with "reality as an object of thought" is *realitas objectiva,* which (for obvious reasons) many translate with "objective reality." In fact, in Latin as in English, the terms *subjective* and *objective* exchanged meanings around the middle of the seventeenth century, and the phrase "objective reality" is therefore misleading as a translation for *realitas objectiva:* some of the things that have *realitas objectiva* exist subjectively, not objectively, in the modern senses of those terms. I have therefore tended to avoid the phrase "objective reality."

14. Three of these times, it appears in the phrase "formally or eminently," in contexts in which Descartes is not concerned with distinguishing the eminent from the formal (AT 7:41, 42, 46). The fourth time, it appears in a brief discussion of the hypothesis (later rejected) that even if he were not extended in space, he might still have spatial extension in him eminently and so might be the author of his ideas of bodies (AT 7:45). The only other mention of eminent reality in the *Meditations* is in a passage in *Meditation VI* in which Descartes considers (and ultimately rejects) the thought that his ideas of bodies are caused in him by "one of God's creatures" that, though not itself spatial, contains spatial extension in itself eminently (AT 7:79).

15. For a discussion of Descartes' views on these matters, see Brian E. O'Neil, *Epistemological Direct Realism in Descartes' Philosophy* (Albuquerque: University of New Mexico Press, 1974). O'Neil discusses the passage from *Replies I* about the sun on page 71.

16. George Berkeley, *Three Dialogues between Hylas and Philonous,* ed. David Hilbert and John Perry (Claremont, Calif.: Areté Press, 1994), 40.

17. Of course, the formal/objective distinction does not straightforwardly reduce to the physical/mental distinction. Properties can be present in our minds formally as well as objectively, and the object of a thought may itself be a mental entity.

18. Compare J. E. K. Secada, "Descartes on Time and Causality," *Philosophi-*

cal Review 94, no. 1 (January 1990): 45–72. Secada's own view is that, as far as we can tell from Descartes' writings, he had no beliefs about the continuity or discontinuity of time (46).

19. This principle must have been especially attractive to people, including many of Descartes' contemporaries, who believed that a first physical entity cannot directly move a second unless the first comes into spatial contact with the second.

20. Kenny asks, "Why may not each time slice be the cause of the existence of the next, dying phoenix-like in giving birth to its successor?" (*Descartes,* 144). Descartes' answer, I suspect, has to do with continued existence. We say that the same phoenix is present before and after the rebirth partly because we take there to be something (or, at any rate, some stuff) that was there all through the transformation—something that is a bird, then a pile of ashes, and then a bird again. But, once we have divided time into nonoverlapping moments (and agreed to view "enduring" objects as constructions out of temporal object slices), we seem to preclude our saying that something (other than a construction out of temporal parts) remains as we move from moment to moment.

21. *Summa Theologica,* part 1, question 2, article 3. See, for instance, *Readings in Medieval Philosophy,* ed. Andrew B. Schoedinger (Oxford: Oxford University Press, 1996), 65.

22. See, for example, *Confessions,* book 10, chap. 27: "You [God] were within me, and I was in the world outside myself." St. Augustine, *Confessions,* trans. R. S. Pine Coffin (Baltimore: Penguin, 1973), 231.

CHAPTER 6

1. Descartes' view, familiar from Neoplatonism, is that the universe is better with imperfect parts in it than it would be without them. Fullness, completeness, and continuity are good, and they seem to require that each place in which there might be an entity be filled. But, according to Descartes, the possible places for entities form a line extending from God's full being to nonexistence (AT 7:54). For God's creation to be perfect, he argues, there must be beings all along this line. That is, for the creation to be perfect, it must contain imperfect things.

2. This is in fact a Gnostic view (which derives in part from Plato's *Timeas*). For example, according to one of the Gnostic gospels, "The Secret Book According to John," the primary Godhead creates a realm of eternal beings, who then produce Ialtabaoth—a monstrous offspring who intentionally designs humans so as to hide important truths from us. On this story, the Godhead is not responsible for our errors, but we do not bear full responsibility either. See *The Gnostic Scriptures,* trans. Bentley Layton (Garden City, N.Y.: Doubleday, 1987), 28–51. In the same volume, compare "The Reality of the Rulers," 68–76.

3. I introduced this term, which now seems to be in common use, in "Descartes's Validation of Clear and Distinct Apprehension," *Philosophical Review* 86 (1977): 197–208. The interpretation of Descartes' strategy presented in this section appeared in that essay.

4. Harry G. Frankfurt, *Demons, Dreamers, and Madmen: The Defense of Reason in Descartes' Meditations* (New York: Bobbs-Merrill, 1970), 25.

5. The Demon's Advocate will speak up again because (i) the arguments of *Meditations III* and *IV* only make the hypothesis of the evil demon seem nonsensical to Descartes while he keeps those arguments in mind, and (ii) Descartes does not attempt explicitly to refute the dream hypothesis until *Meditation VI*.

6. Anthony Kenny, *Descartes: A Study of His Philosophy* (New York: Random House, 1968), 195.

7. Frankfurt, *Demons*, 180.

8. Gary Hatfield, "The Cartesian Circle," in *The Blackwell Guide to Descartes' Meditations*, ed. Stephen Gaukroger (Oxford: Blackwell, 2006), 134.

9. While admitting that the "psychological interpretation" of the *Meditations* has "considerable textual merit," Louis E. Loeb still worries that, if it is correct, Descartes' strategy may "depend upon an accidental or contingent fact of human psychology." See Loeb, "The Cartesian Circle," in *The Cambridge Companion to Descartes*, ed. John Cottingham (Cambridge: Cambridge University Press, 1992), 235. But would Descartes say that it just happens to be the case, as a matter of psychological fact, that our Understandings compel our Wills to affirm that 2 + 3 = 5? After completing *Meditation IV*'s argument to the conclusion that our minds are reliable instruments for detecting truth, he can say that the fact that our Understandings compel our Wills to affirm the proposition "2 + 3 = 5" has to do *both* with the psychological connection between our Understandings and our Wills *and* with the truth value of that proposition—just as the fact that a reliable scale reads "one hundred pounds" has to do both with the mechanism of the scale and with the weight of the object placed on that scale.

CHAPTER 7

1. Being somewhat taller than average, I cannot prevent myself from believing that my head is going to hit the supports on wooden roller coasters, even though I know that the coasters would have been shut down or modified if that were the case.

2. Margaret Wilson, *Descartes* (Boston: Routledge & Kegan Paul, 1978), 79.

3. There are, however, assent compellers, such as "The past cannot be altered," whose comprehension does not seem to involve the clear and distinct idea of any entities.

4. See Descartes, *The Philosophical Writings of Descartes*, ed. John Cotting-

ham, Robert Stoothoff, and Dugald Murdock (Cambridge: Cambridge University Press, 1984), 215, n. 1.

5. Spinoza seems to identify an object with its essence even more explicitly than Descartes. The essence of an object *x,* says Spinoza in definition 2 of part 2 of the *Ethics,* is that which is present whenever *x* is present and absent whenever *x* is absent—that of which we conceive when and only when we conceive of *x.* Spinoza, *Ethics,* trans. Samuel Shirley (Indianapolis: Hackett, 1991), 79. The only thing that bears this relation to *x* is, I suggest, *x* itself.

CHAPTER 8

1. A variant of the argument appears in *Replies II* (AT 7:166–67), where—rather than saying that it pertains to God's nature to exist—Descartes says that necessary existence is contained in the concept [*conceptus*] of God.

2. Alan Gewirth, "The Cartesian Circle," *Philosophical Review* 50 (1941): 368.

CHAPTER 9

1. Far from claiming novelty for his views, Descartes here says that, in presenting his arguments for dualism, he was following the directives of a Church council (Fifth Lateran, eighth session, 1513), which had urged Christian philosophers to refute the view that the soul dies with the body (AT 7:3).

2. Arnauld objects that, since Descartes infers his existence from the single fact that he thinks, it's no surprise that he forms the idea of himself as simply a thinking thing (*Objections IV,* AT 7:203), but Descartes responds that, however he has arrived at the idea of himself as a *res cogitans,* the fact remains that he does have this idea (*Replies IV,* AT 7:227).

3. When Henri de Roi, who had been a student of Descartes', broke with his teacher, he published a list of the points on which they disagreed. Descartes' *Comments on a Certain Broadside* (1648) was his reply to de Roi.

4. In the *Principles,* Descartes maintains that a thing's essence is its "principle attribute"—a property that all the thing's other properties presuppose (*Princ. I,* 53, AT 8:25). Accordingly, if he could show that modes of his mind—such as the ability to have mental images—do not presuppose extension, he could infer that his body is not the substance in which such modes reside and hence that there must be a substance of another sort in which they do reside. See Marleen Rozemond, *Descartes' Dualism* (Cambridge, Mass.: Harvard University Press, 1988), 1–37. But, while Descartes' principles may provide him with the material for this argument, it does not seem to me to that he did argue this way in *Meditation VI.* Neither the passage containing the primary argument in *Meditation VI* nor Des-

cartes' summary of that argument in *Replies II* mentions any properties, modes, or abilities of *M*. Also, while Descartes does frequently use the term *essence* in the *Meditations,* and while he may have in hand an argument to the conclusion that every property of an entity depends on that entity's essence (Chapter 7), the phrase "principle property" does not appear anywhere in Descartes' argument for dualism in *Meditation VI*, and he does not even hint there at the thesis that each of a thing's properties presupposes that thing's essence.

5. As I argued in Chapter 1, the Demon's Advocate cannot sincerely assert the negations of propositions like "2 + 3 = 5," since those negations do not seem to him to make sense. But he can assert the negation of the proposition "There is a physical world," since the proposition itself is not one that his Understanding compels his Will to affirm.

6. Compare the very first sentence of Descartes' *Treatise on Man* (AT 11:199–200), in which he says that humans are composed of both souls and bodies.

7. Gilbert Ryle, *The Concept of Mind* (New York: Harper & Row, 1949), 15–16. The title of the book's first chapter is in fact "Descartes' Myth."

CHAPTER 10

1. When Descartes lays out the reasoning of the *Meditations* in a "geometrical manner" at the end of *Replies II,* he stops with the argument that the mind is distinct from the body without even mentioning this validation or his argument to the conclusion that there is a physical world.

2. See Cecilia Wee, "Descartes' Two Proofs of the External World," *Australasian Journal of Philosophy* 80, no. 4 (December 2002): 487–501.

3. Unlike the argument in *Meditation VI,* the argument in the *Principles* does not rest on the premise that, if our ideas of sensible things came from something other than physical objects, there would be no way for us to discover that fact. Also, in the *Principles,* there is no explicit mention of the "strong inclinations" on which the argument of *Meditation VI* centers. Yet both arguments begin from the observation that we passively receive ideas from outside ourselves, both appeal to premises about where such ideas *seem* to come from, and both rest crucially on the thought that God is not deceptive.

4. In *Meditation VI,* Descartes notes that a person who is inclined by a sensation of pain to affirm that there is something wrong with his foot may later discover that the damage is really to the nerves connecting the foot to the brain (AT 7:88). Some have taken this as an example of a case in which a person discovers that a proposition he was strongly inclined to believe is false. But, while the example is suggestive, the inclination here may not be quite the same as the

"strong inclination" to affirm that physical objects exist, since it may not arise in what Descartes calls the "third stage of sensation."

5. There is another problem concerning the criteria for being a deceiver, less immediately relevant to the evaluation of the argument under consideration. Suppose my acquaintance tells me that he was born in Ohio and that, as a result, I come to hold the (false) belief that he was born there. As we ordinarily wield the concept of deception, it's no defense against the accusation of deceit that, by searching through birth certificates, I could in theory have discovered the true location of his birth.

6. Compare Descartes, *The Philosophical Writings of Descartes,* ed. John Cottingham, Robert Stoothoff, and Dugald Murdock (Cambridge: Cambridge University Press, 1984), 55.

7. This tactic will not work in the *Principles,* however, since Descartes' locution there is "*Deus non est deceptor*" rather than "*Deus non est fallax.*"

References

Augustine. *Confessions.* Translated by R. S. Pine Coffin. Baltimore: Penguin, 1973.

Berkeley, George. *Three Dialogues between Hylas and Philonous.* Edited by David Hilbert and John Perry. Claremont, Calif.: Areté Press, 1994.

Boethius. *Philosophiae Consolationis.* Edited by Karl Buchner. Heidelberg: Winter, 1977.

Broughton, Janet. *Descartes's Method of Doubt.* Princeton, N.J.: Princeton University Press, 2003.

Descartes, René. *Oeuvres de Descartes.* Edited by Charles Adam and Paul Tannery. Paris: Leopold Cerf, 1904. Vols. 7, 8A, and 10.

————. *The Philosophical Writings of Descartes.* Translated by John Cottingham, Robert Stoothoff, and Dugald Murdoch. Cambridge: Cambridge University Press, 1984, vols. 1 and 2.

Doney, Willis, ed. *Descartes: A Collection of Critical Essays.* Notre Dame: University of Notre Dame Press, 1968.

Cottingham, John, ed. *The Cambridge Companion to Descartes.* Cambridge: Cambridge University Press, 1992.

Curley, Edwin M. *Descartes against the Skeptics.* Oxford: Blackwell, 1978.

Frankfurt, Harry G. *Demons, Dreamers, and Madmen: The Defense of Reason in Descartes' Meditations.* New York: Bobbs-Merrill, 1970.

Gewirth, Alan. "The Cartesian Circle." *Philosophical Review* 50 (1941): 368–95.

Hatfield, Gary. "The Cartesian Circle." In *The Blackwell Guide to Descartes' Meditations.* Edited by Stephen Gaukroger. Oxford: Blackwell, 2006.

Hintikka, Jaaco. "Cogito, Ergo Sum: Inference or Performance." In *Descartes: A Collection of Critical Essays,* edited by Willis Doney, 108–39. Notre Dame: University of Notre Dame Press, 1968.

Kenny, Anthony. *Descartes: A Study of His Philosophy.* New York: Random House, 1968.

Kuhn, Thomas. *The Copernican Revolution: Planetary Astronomy in the Development of Western Thought.* Cambridge, Mass.: Harvard University Press, 1957.

Layton, Bentley, trans. *The Gnostic Scriptures.* Garden City, N.Y.: Doubleday, 1987.

Locke, John. *An Essay Concerning Human Understanding.* Edited by A. C. Fraser. New York: Dover, 1959.

Loeb, Louis E. "The Cartesian Circle." In Cottingham, *Cambridge Companion to Descartes.*

O'Neil, Brian E. *Epistemological Direct Realism in Descartes' Philosophy.* Albuquerque: University of New Mexico Press, 1974.

Popkin, Richard H. *The History of Scepticism from Erasmus to Spinoza.* Berkeley: University of California Press, 1979.

Rozemond, Marleen. *Descartes' Dualism.* Cambridge, Mass.: Harvard University Press, 1988.

Rubin, Ronald. "Descartes's Validation of Clear and Distinct Apprehension." *Philosophical Review* 86 (1977): 197–208.

———. Reviews of Curley's *Descartes against the Skeptics* and Williams' *Descartes: The Project of Pure Enquiry.* British Journal for the Philosophy of Science 31 (1980): 104–8.

Ryle, Gilbert. *The Concept of Mind.* New York: Harper & Row, 1949.

Schoedinger, Andrew B., ed. *Readings in Medieval Philosophy.* Oxford: Oxford University Press, 1996.

Secada, J. E. K. "Descartes on Time and Causality." *Philosophical Review* 94, no. 1 (January 1990): 45–72.

Sextus Empiricus. *Sextus Empiricus: Selections from the Major Writings on Scepticism, Man, and God.* Edited by Philip P. Hallie. Indianapolis: Hackett, 1985.

Spinoza, Baruch. *Ethics.* Translated by Samuel Shirley. Indianapolis: Hackett, 1991.

Suarez, Francisco. *Disputationes Metaphysicae I.* Hildensheim: Georg Olms, 1965.

Wee, Cecilia. "Descartes' Two Proofs of the External World." *Australasian Journal of Philosophy* 80, no. 4 (December 2002): 487–501.

Williams, Bernard. *Descartes: The Project of Pure Enquiry.* Sussex: Harvester Press, 1978.

Wilson, Margaret. *Descartes.* Boston: Routledge & Kegan Paul, 1978.

Woolhouse, R. S. *Descartes, Spinoza, Leibniz: The Concept of Substance in Seventeenth Century Metaphysics.* New York: Routledge, 1993.

Index